EDUCATION IN CANADA

World Education Series

World Education Series

General Editors: Michael D. Stephens
MA, MEd, PhD, FRGS

Gordon W. Roderick
BSc, MA, PhD, MInstP

Education in
Canada

JOSEPH KATZ
Professor of Comparative Education and
Chairman of the Department of Curriculum,
University of British Columbia

DAVID & CHARLES   *Newton Abbot*

ARCHON BOOKS   *Hamden, Connecticut*
1974

These pages are dedicated to my parents
whose love of life and learning helped Canada
on its way to a heritage of humanity.

This edition first published 1974 in Great Britain by
David & Charles (Holdings) Limited, Newton Abbot, Devon
and in the United States of America by Archon Books,
an imprint of The Shoe String Press, Inc, Hamden, Connecticut 06514

ISBN 0 7153 6294 1 (Great Britain)
ISBN 0 208 01446 2 (United States)

Set in eleven on thirteen point Imprint
and printed in Great Britain
by Latimer Trend & Company Ltd Plymouth

Contents

Foreword

CANADA has the distinction of being the only advanced nation in the world without a federal office of education. At a time in history when national perspectives are essential to the determination of a national identity, when planning on a national level is crucial to national development and when a national voice is needed in the international community, the Canadian peoples as a whole are without this kind of educational direction.

The fact that there are national organisations concerned with education, such as the Canadian Teachers Federation, the Canadian School Trustees Association, the Canadian Education Association and its creature the Council of Ministers of Education, as well as others, only serves to illustrate the tacit recognition of the need for a national office. As it is, education, still looked upon by the provinces as their exclusive jurisdiction, is provincially oriented, controlled and determined. At a period in history when education is acknowledged to be as important to the life of a nation as economics and politics, provincial and federal politicians in Canada have permitted education to fall between federal and provincial political stools; many critics feel it has become a divisive rather than a unifying institution.

As a result of this the Canadian peoples have been forced to rely on the products of educational systems other than their own. Because there is no central office of education in Canada to collect and disseminate information about Canadian education, Canadian educators, to say nothing of those abroad, can be unaware of what is happening in Canadian education. Canadian students may be

7

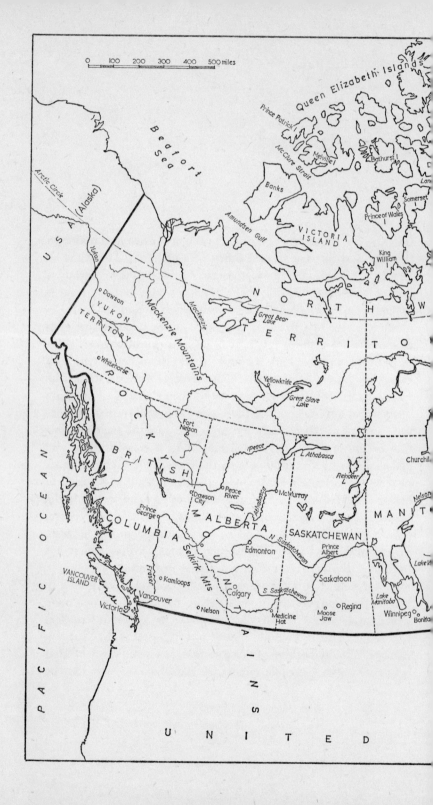

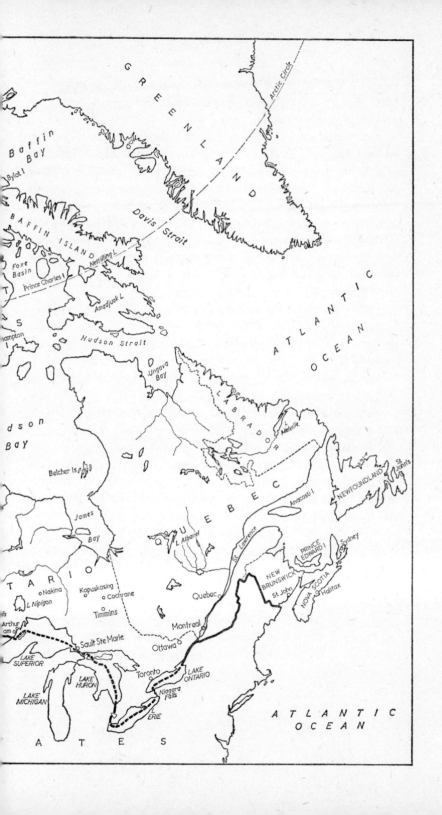

taught by teachers and professors who have little acquaintance with the Canadian ethos or with its cultural, academic and professional conventions.

The pages which follow describe the public and private educational systems to be found in Canada. These systems, despite the problems mentioned earlier, are remarkably similar one to another, a fact which attests their common European and American heritage, and such differences as there are may be attributed not only to the accidents of history and geography but to the influences exerted by the two founding nations, the French and the British, and to the educational aspirations of the many different nationalities that came over the years to make Canada their home.

The four centuries during which Canada's educational systems evolved were witness to dramatic changes in the social, economic, political and religious character of the country. Confederation brought with it a sense of destiny. The westward movement of civilisation flowed in Canada from the Atlantic to the Pacific and in the process was enriched by the perspectives of new groups of pioneers who helped to build the new world on the cultural and educational foundations of the old.

Canada's schools, colleges and universities, both public and private, are witness to the vision of pioneer and immigrant in placing their faith in education. They came to Canada seeking opportunities and a better way of life for themselves and their children. They found their hopes realised in the new horizons of their day. But today is another day, and today's youth see their horizons in the world and the universe. Today's youth in Canada can only become tomorrow's Canadian and world citizens if their schools, colleges and universities are rooted in an educational ethos that is not bounded by the limited perspectives of provincial boundaries. A Canadian ethos can only be cultivated by a Canadian office of education that stands as a beacon to youth and helps them to see themselves and their country in the context of one world and one humanity.

J.K.

Canada

HISTORICAL SURVEY

THE discovery and exploration of what is now Canada was begun by Leif Ericsson in the year 1000 and was continued by Cabot in 1497, Cartier who sailed the St Lawrence in 1534, Champlain who founded Quebec in 1608, Hudson who gave his name to Hudson Bay in 1609. Radisson and Groseilliers reached the west in 1660, Kelsey the far west in 1690, Samuel Hearne the northwest in 1769, and Alexander Mackenzie crossed the continent to reach the Pacific in 1793. The early period of exploration established the French in the northern part of the continent until 1763, when hegemony passed to Britain.

During the century and a half of French rule, Quebec was established by Champlain, schools and hospitals were started by religious orders, and settlement and industry were initiated, especially by Talon. The west was explored by, among others, La Verendrye and his sons. By 1763, when France and England signed the Peace of Paris ceding Canada to England, the French language and culture had been thoroughly established in both its civil and ecclesiastical institutions. Thenceforward French custom and convention were to play a significant role in the shaping of Canada.

Between 1763 and 1867 British parliamentary government was established. The trek of peoples from Europe to Canada increased. Samuel Hearne, David Thompson and Alexander Mackenzie pushed Canada's horizon westward and northward, and westward trade and settlement were extended. By 1811 there

was a settlement on the Red and Assiniboine rivers in what was
later to become Manitoba, and settlers' trails had left their marks
across the prairies as far as Alberta. During this period, too, the
peoples settled in present-day Ontario and Quebec, respectively
Upper Canada and Lower Canada, reached for political accommodation in the Quebec Act of 1774, the Constitutional Act of
1791, and the Act of Union in 1841. In 1864, when the Charlotte-
town Conference brought the Fathers of Confederation together
to explore their common interests, it became clear that four
provinces, Nova Scotia, New Brunswick, Quebec and Ontario,
saw the advantages of confederation: this was given them by the
British North America Act of 1867, which also provided for the
later entry of other areas of Canada.

The peoples of Canada who did not share in this vision of the
future were the native Indians on the one hand and the Eskimos
on the other. The battles which had been fought between the
Indians and the French and English had resulted in the ultimate
segregation of the Indians on reservations which took them
effectively out of the mainstream of development, a miscarriage
of justice which has only recently begun to be corrected. The
Eskimos were left to pursue their ancient way of life, hunting
and fishing, until Canada's explorations for oils and minerals in
the far north began to open other opportunities to them, not
always to their advantage.

The period between the establishment of confederation in 1867
and the first decade of the twentieth century witnessed the entry
into confederation of Manitoba (1870), British Columbia (1871),
Prince Edward Island (1873), Alberta and Saskatchewan (1905);
Newfoundland did not enter until 1949. During this period the
Intercolonial Railway was completed (1876), the Canadian
Pacific Railway linked the west coast to the rest of Canada, and
cable and telephone established communication links between
parts of Canada and between Canada and the rest of the world.

Canada's economic and political maturation concluded with
independence from Britain spelled out in the Statute of West-

minster in 1931. Canada had earlier demonstrated its national viability by its participation in World War I, by becoming a member of the League of Nations in 1919, and by undertaking at a later date an abortive review—the Rowell-Swois Commission—of the British North America Act in 1937. During the 1930s too, Canadians dealt with a depression, absorbed successive waves of migration, established a national broadcasting system, and began a transcontinental air service. By the time Canada participated in World War II Canadians had so developed their natural and human resources that they were then capable of taking their place in the comity of nations. In 1945 Canada became a charter member of the United Nations; in 1946 the Canadian Citizenship Act was passed; in 1951 the Massey Commission brought in a report which resulted in the establishment of the Canada Council in 1957 designed to support the arts, letters and sciences. In 1952 television broadcasting began in Canada.

The next two decades in Canada's story saw social legislation extended to cover old age pensions and medicare. In addition the needs of youth were recognised first in the establishment of the Company of Young Canadians and later in the Opportunity for Youth Programs. This was a period, too, that witnessed a significant increase in urbanisation so that by the seventies the ratio of urban to rural population was 80:20. During this period Canada's Gross National Product doubled and trade with the United States increased over that with Britain. More significant for the future of confederation was the emergence of Quebec's concern with its place in confederation and with the preservation of its culture. Also, the federal government had come to see the value to the nation of giving direct financial assistance to the universities, though this assistance was later channelled through the provincial governments. In this period, too, Canada extended its international aid through the Canadian International Development Agency by assistance to developing countries in the Caribbean, Asia, Africa and Micronesia. By the beginning of the seventies Canada's position in the comity of nations had been considerably enhanced by its adoption of its own distinctive flag, its social welfare programmes, its international commitments and its recognition of the multicultural character of its own society.

GEOGRAPHY

Canada's ten provinces and two territories span some 4,500 miles between the Atlantic and the Pacific oceans and reach from the 49th parallel to the Arctic Ocean, some four million square miles in all. Between the Pacific and Atlantic coasts lie six natural divisions, the Appalachians, the Great Lakes–St Lawrence Lowlands, the Canadian Shield, the Plains, the Western Cordilleras and the Arctic Islands. The climates in these regions range from the soft, relatively mild west coast of the Pacific region through the extremes of the interior continental and Arctic areas.

Among the outstanding geographic features of this vast land is the Great Canadian Shield, which sweeps in a wide arc from western Quebec through southern Ontario and Manitoba and arches across northern Saskatchewan to the Arctic. The shield is the source of many of the minerals which have made Canada one of the world's great mining nations. The prairies, which reach for a thousand miles from Manitoba through Alberta to the Rockies and have been called the breadbasket of the world, are another significant feature. The mountains and valleys of British Columbia constitute yet another geographic feature which determines the character of the economy and society of that area. On the other side of the continent the Atlantic provinces, including Newfoundland, are relatively poor in natural resources and in consequence suffer economically.

Rich as Canada's land resources are, its water resources are equally if not more impressive. In addition to the three oceans which wash its shores it has large freshwater lakes in Ontario, Manitoba, British Columbia and the Northwest Territories. Its river systems are among the greatest in the world and include the St Lawrence, the Mackenzie, the Fraser and the Columbia, to name only a few. Niagara Falls and Hudson Bay are other famous and valuable water resources. These systems of rivers and lakes have provided Canada not only with a vast communication and transportation system but have also provided for vast power resources necessary to industrial and commercial development.

THE FIRST SCHOOLS

The Indians and Eskimos of what is now Canada had educational practices which contributed to the maintenance and modification of their respective cultures. The elders of these peoples ensured the transference of their ways of life to their young people, and did so both economically and efficiently. The transition from infancy to youth and later to adulthood was marked in each instance by well-defined requirements established in custom and convention. The fact that the system was sufficient to produce the necessary leadership for peace and war attests its efficacy for the times.

The educational practices of the native peoples of Canada were ignored in the course of the development of the formal educational systems introduced by church and state and it was not until after World War II that Indian and Eskimo language and culture began to find a place in formal schooling.

The religious orders were the first to establish formal schools in Canada, often in association with their church activities and their attempts to convert the natives to Christianity. The earliest such schools were established by the Recollects and Jesuits in Quebec in the first quarter of the seventeenth century. During the seventeenth and eighteenth centuries the westward flow of education also began with the religious orders. The establishment of schools by the Recollects and Jesuits in Quebec in 1608, the Ursuline Convent for girls in 1639, a school in Bonavista, Newfoundland, 1726, the Rev John Stuart Academy

in Quebec in 1781, Provencher in Manitoba in 1818, and St
Anne's Mission in Alberta in 1842. Schools were also established
and maintained throughout the West, many of which still continue.

The French influence was matched by the British Society for
the Propagation of the Gospel in Foreign Parts, whose members
established schools in New Brunswick, Nova Scotia and Newfoundland. In addition, there were schools conducted by itinerant
schoolmasters, usually returned soldiers, and usually in remote
areas where several families banded together to take turns in
boarding the teachers for the benefit of their children.

The religious orders continue to play a part in education by
maintaining separate or denominational schools in most provinces alongside the state school system. In the Northwest
Territories, particularly, the schools maintained by the religious
orders have played and still do play a most important part.
However, here as elsewhere the economics of education and the
decline in the numbers of lay and religious teachers available to
these systems are contributing to their decline.

STATE SCHOOLS

The eighteenth and nineteenth centuries in Canada witnessed
the rapid growth of public (state) school systems, this development following the emergence of the political entities which
were ultimately to become the Canadian Confederation. Newfoundland passed an Act in 1876 providing for denominational
school boards. Nova Scotia as early as 1766 had required that
teachers should be examined by the local clergy. In 1808 Nova
Scotia passed an Act providing for education through a real and
property tax and called for free education in an Act of 1811.
Prince Edward Island set land aside for schools in 1767 and had
a Free Education Act by 1852. New Brunswick ruled in 1816
that there be a grammar school in each county. An Act for Free
Schools was passed in Quebec in 1801 and in 1824 the Fabrique
Act set aside land in the province for school purposes. Ontario

had a Grammar Schools Act in 1807, a Common Schools Act in 1816, an Act providing for boards of education in 1823, and schools were made free in 1870. Manitoba had a Public Schools Act in 1871 and by 1908 had a minister of education. The territories which were later, in 1905, to become Alberta and Saskatchewan had a Council of Public Instruction in 1892 and compulsory education laws in 1889 which stipulated among other things that children between the ages of seven and twelve had to attend schools for at least twelve weeks a year. British Columbia tried to introduce free—ie no fees were required—schools in an Act of 1865 which proved abortive, but did have an Ordinance for Public Schools in 1869 and a Public Schools Act in 1872, a year after entering confederation. From the foregoing it is obvious that education loomed large in the minds of Canada's earliest settlers and that despite the harsh conditions of life under primitive circumstances they recognised the necessity of giving it priority of place.

THE DEVELOPMENT OF SCHOOL SYSTEMS

Since the turn of the century Canada has witnessed the consolidation, expansion, modernisation and diversification of its educational systems. Provincial departments of education were organised and reorganised to meet changing and increasing needs. The federal government began to perceive its responsibility for stimulating the development of educational programmes not possible of perception by provincial authorities, as in the case of health and physical educational, and vocational and technical, training. These years, too, witnessed the lengthening of the school year from a few weeks to approximately 200 days. School climates changed to reflect and accommodate the new theories of education stemming from a deeper understanding of childhood and a more scientific approach to the education process. The curricula of elementary and secondary schools were modified and extended to include a variety of studies including social studies, art, music and physical education at the elementary level,

B

and vocational, technical and commercial subjects at the secondary.

Teacher-training programmes were extended much beyond the high school to reach university-level studies. Teachers' organisations came into being to further the interests of the teaching profession and in that way bring about an improvement in education generally. School buildings were much improved to reflect the broader role of education in the life of the child: library facilities, cafeterias, gymnasia, counselling rooms, music and art studies, and very extensive playing fields were added to some schools.

These changes in Canadian education reflected changes which took place in the United States, Europe and Britain, but they also reflected the fact that Canada had advanced socially, economically and politically to the point where its educational systems had to keep abreast of changing times.

POLITICAL DIVISIONS

The ten provinces and two territories which constitute the political divisions of Canada are the Atlantic Provinces (Newfoundland, Nova Scotia, Prince Edward Island and New Brunswick), Quebec, Ontario, the Prairies (Manitoba, Saskatchewan and Alberta), British Columbia, the Yukon and the Northwest Territories. These political divisions emerged not only because of the social and cultural bonds which determined each local group's history but because geography and economics also welded them into clearly defined entities. Thus the British texture of Ontario contrasts sharply with the French texture of Quebec, and both with the mixture that constitutes the Atlantic Provinces, and with the cosmopolitan character of the Prairies.

The tensions which characterise federal-provincial relations to some extent reflect the underlying social, economic, political and religious fabric of the regions as well as of the individual provinces. The federal government is called upon at regular intervals to redress the balance between east and west and north and south: to help equalise the economic poverty of the Atlantic

Provinces with the economic wealth of British Columbia; to have the agricultural west reconciled to the industrial east; and to have the south realise that the northern part of Canada needs development. Within this political and economic context it is difficult to expect any kind of uniform educational policy to develop or to avoid some great disparities in educational policies and expenditures.

ECONOMY

The products of the farm, the forest, the mine and the sea have traditionally constituted the baseline for the Canadian economy. However, since World Wars I and II the economy has become industrialised, with at least one person in three in the manufacturing work force.

The economics of the country vary widely. The forests of British Columbia and Quebec provide the resources for the lumber and pulp and paper industries. The mines of British Columbia, Ontario, Manitoba, Saskatchewan and Labrador contribute significantly to Canada's internal and external trade. Both the Atlantic and Pacific provinces have heavy investment in the fishing industry. The agricultural productivity of the west and to some extent of Ontario and British Columbia is well known.

Canadian secondary industry was slow in developing, primarily because of its small local market potential but essentially because the economy had capitalised on the ease with which it could produce primary products and find a world market for them. Canadian dependence for manufactured items first on Britain and second on the United States also limited industrial development. However, Canada's participation in two world wars and the emergence of important industries such as pulp and paper, lumber, machinery, iron and steel, chemicals, aluminium, milling, canning, brewing and shipbuilding changed the character of the Canadian economy from the predominantly agricultural to the essentially industrial. With the increase in the industrial work force came greater urbanisation, and development in

vocational, technical and technological education. The needs of
industry for technical skills of all sorts resulted in considerable
expansion in this branch of education at intermediate and senior
levels. These needs also pointed to the fact that many more
scientific research and development programmes were necessary
if industry was to be developed still further.

A secondary effect has been an increasing awareness that if the
scientific and technological knowhow of its young people is to
be put to use in Canada and a brain-and-skill drain avoided, then
a far more aggressive policy of industrial development must be
followed. The development of even more secondary industries
would make it possible for Canada to utilise its own human and
natural resources to good advantage without shipping them abroad.

POPULATION

Canada's approximately 23 million people live mainly within the
100 miles north of the 49th parallel and are distributed through
the provinces in roughly the following proportions: 8 million
in Ontario, 7 million in Quebec, 4 million in the Prairies, 2
million in the Atlantic Provinces, 2 million in British Columbia
and 75,000 in the two northern territories. Population density
overall is of the order of 6 persons per square mile. On the other
hand about 80 per cent of Canada's population live in urban
centres with well over half concentrated in some 20 major cities.
There are in the overall population about 35 different national
and religious groupings.

The past decade has witnessed a significant change in the
character of the Canadian population stemming from the introduction of revised immigration laws. These revisions provided for
what is called skills-only immigration. In 1968 the following report
indicated the results of this change in policy:

> Canada last year attracted more skilled and professional immi-
> grant talent than many countries possess in their entire popula-
> tion. And the total immigration, 223,000, was exceeded in only
> six years of the last 100 years.

This welcome inflow included 4,000 ready-made engineers, 1,300 physical scientists, 2,000 professors and principals, 5,400 school teachers, 1,200 doctors and 4,300 graduate nurses . . . and 800 artists, writers and musicians.

. . . In the 10-year period between 1946–1955 the total number of immigrants with professional standing was 44,500. In 1967 alone, immigrants with professions numbered 31,000.

The Financial Post (18 March 1968)

The character of this immigration pattern exerts an influence on educational development by virtue of the natural expectations which these people have for their children in coming to Canada.

CULTURES

Although Canada is officially a bilingual and bicultural society based on the fact that the English and the French were the two founding peoples, it is in reality a multicultural society, the Canadian Mosaic, in which peoples from all of the continents of the world are represented: Englishmen, Irishmen, Scots, Welshmen, Albanians, Austrians, Belgians, Bulgarians, Czechs and Slovaks, Estonians, Finns, French, Germans, Greeks, Hungarians, Italians, Jews, Latvians, Lithuanians, Luxemburgers, Maltese, Netherlanders, Poles, Portuguese, Rumanians, Russians, Danes, Icelanders, Norwegians, Swedes, Spaniards, Swiss, Ukranians, Yugoslavians, Arabs, Armenians, Chinese, East Indians, Japanese, Lebanese, Mexicans, Negroes, Syrians, Turks, in addition to the native Indians and Eskimos. The classrooms of the nation, with few exceptions, contain a cross-section of several of these cultural groups, with the result that the basic social referent for the teachers is essentially a multicultural one. Over the years, and depending upon the rate of immigration, an increasing proportion of each classroom has been made up of first, second, and third generation Canadians, a circumstance which contributes to shaping that elusive dimension, the Canadian identity.

Approximately 45 per cent of the population are British in

origin, 30 per cent French and the remainder from the host of countries indicated above. The 25 per cent of the population whose native languages are other than English or French have, by virtue of a new appreciation of the value of a diversity of cultures in the society, come to play a more important part in public policy making. This change in the social and political climate has led to Canada's educational institutions modifying their school, college and university curricula to provide for new views and values.

NATIONAL INFLUENCES

Canada's schools, colleges and universities have of course been shaped in part by the impact of educational theories and practices derived from Scotland, England, France, and the United States. The early explorers and adventurers, the militia and the missionaries, and later the settlers and the businessmen, came from Britain, Europe and the United States and brought with them ideas about church and state and education which they adapted to their local situations.

The Scottish influence has been well documented by Andrew Skinner, who pointed out the signal contributions made by John Dawson, one-time superintendent of education in Nova Scotia and later principal of McGill University, Alexander Shakel who was associated with the Protestant high school of Montreal, Dr Thomas McCulloch whose school became Pictou Academy, David Stowe whose ideas on leader training helped set a pattern for Canada's efforts in this direction, and George Paxton Young who helped reform secondary education in Ontario and, of course, Egerton Ryerson who built the educational structure of Ontario which serves as model to western Canadian educational development. There were in addition many Scottish educators, such as J. S. Little of Winnipeg, who brought educational ideas shaped in Edinburgh. Furthermore, Scottish influence helped develop the universities of Dalhousie, Queen's, Alberta, Manitoba and McGill.

The French influence on Canadian education is evident in the existence of Quebec and in the French-speaking communities located elsewhere throughout Canada, particularly in New Brunswick, Ontario and Manitoba. From the sixteenth century onwards French logic, literature, music, and philosophy have influenced Canada's educational theories and practices. The *collège classique* of Quebec, the adherence to a classical tradition in the humanities, and men of the calibre of Etienne Gilson, Jean-Paul Viney, Louis Philippe Audet, Lionel Desjarlais, Arthur Godbout and Anthony Paplauskas-Ramunas have all exercised a profound influence on education in Canada.

England's contribution to the development of Canadian education lay in the sending of well-qualified missionaries and teachers in the early days and at a later date such outstanding educators as Peter Sandiford and R. A. Fisher, to mention only two of a long list prepared by Willard Brehaut. Furthermore, the vesting of exclusive jurisdiction for education in the provinces may be attributed to England's influence, and also the practice of appointing royal commissions to deal with pressing social problems including education.

American influences on Canadian education were early, many and varied, and they continue. Apart from the fact that a great many Canadian professionals pursued their graduate and postgraduate work in the United States, there has also been the long, sustained and continuing influence of American news media and publications, including textbooks. Canadian educators have borrowed heavily from American philosophies of education, curricula, methodologies and technologies. Canadian schools, colleges and universities are organised and administered in many instances on principles originating in the United States.

In addition to the foregoing four major influences on Canadian education, there are the views and values of the many cultural groups in Canada whose children attend school, and who express their views through participation in home and school associations as well as other community organisations.

2

Government and Education

LEGISLATION

SECTION 93 of the British North America Act 1867 allocated exclusive jurisdiction for the administration of education to provincial legislatures. The relevant clause reads:

In and for each Province the Legislature may exclusively make laws in relation to Education, subject and according to the following provisions:

(1) Nothing in any such law shall prejudicially affect any Right or Privilege with respect to Denominational Schools which any Class of Persons have by law in the Province at the Union:

(2) All the Powers, Privileges and Duties at the Union by law conferred and imposed in Upper Canada on the Separate Schools and School Trustees of the Queen's Roman Catholic Subjects shall be and the same are hereby extended to the Dissentient Schools of the Queen's Protestant and Roman Catholic Subjects in Quebec:

(3) Where in any Province a System of Separate or Dissentient Schools exists by Law at the Union or is thereafter established by the Legislature of the Province, an Appeal shall lie to the Governor General in Council from any Act or Decision of any Provincial Authority affecting any Right or Privilege of the Protestant or Roman Catholic Minority of the Queen's Subjects in relation to Education:

(4) In case any such Provincial Law as from Time to Time seems to the Governor General in Council requisite for the due Execution of the Provisions of this Section is not made, or in case any Decision of the Governor General in Council on any Appeal under this Section is not duly executed by the proper Provincial Authority in that Behalf, then and in every such Case,

and as far only as the Circumstances of each Case require, the Parliament of Canada may make remedial Laws for the due Execution of the Provisions of this Section and of any Decision of the Governor General in Council under this Section.

E. A. Driedger, *A Consolidation of the British North America Act, 1867–1952* (Ottawa: Queen's Printer, 1956), pp 28–9

It is this legislation, including some modifications to accommodate the entry of Manitoba, Alberta and Newfoundland into confederation, that has made it possible for provincial governments to deny the federal government its rightful place in furthering educational developments to the extent possible. The Canadian Council of Ministers of Education is an example of provincialism, this organisation having been created essentially to preserve provincial interests in education; it is fairly generally agreed today that what is needed is an Office of Education with both national and international perspectives. The fact of the matter is that the provisions of the North America Act, including those for education, are no longer adequate for the needs of society and are consequently serving to inhibit development.

The provisions for separate schools have ensured the educational rights of denominational groups where these were obtained at the time of union (eg Quebec and Ontario), and at the same time established a precedent for others to follow, given provincial readiness to so do. The absence of a state church in Canada has contributed to a flexible approach to accommodating the educational views of parents without jeopardising the role of the state. In a way the separate and provincial systems are looked upon as complementary rather than competitive, and they are indeed moving towards integration as in Ontario and New Brunswick.

Another aspect of federal legislation which influences educational development is the fact that all powers in the British North America Act not specifically allotted to the provinces are reserved to the federal government. It is this residual authority that has enabled the federal government to step in and develop programmes of educational value that lie beyond the provincial jurisdictions' definition of education. The federal government's development of the media, of museums and historical monuments, and its contributions to the arts, letters, sciences and humanities by way of support funds have contributed both directly and indirectly to the development of education in Canada.

ADMINISTRATION

Each province has an elected Minister of Education who is a member of the Cabinet responsible to the Premier and the Legislature. The Cabinet may itself constitute the Council of Public Instruction in some jurisdictions or some other body may serve as the senior policy maker on education in the province. The Minister of Education is responsible for the administration of a department of education and is assisted by a Deputy Minister of Education and one or more Assistant Deputy Ministers. The Deputy Minister of Education is the senior civil servant in the department.

A typical department of education has sections dealing with supervision, inspection, curriculum, elementary education, secondary education, guidance and counselling, audio-visual education, textbooks and libraries, tests and measurements, certification, finance, registration, correspondence and adult education. Some have divisions dealing with higher education and with recreational and community programmes, as well as with museums and cultural activities of various kinds. Not enough have adequate provisions for research and development.

Departments of education are responsible for ensuring that the schools are administered in accordance with the terms of the Schools Act and the departmental regulations. Hence, the department requires school reports from each school district covering teachers, staff, their credentials, student enrolments, attendance records, conduct of the curriculum, examination results, budget provisions, and all related matters. The department certifies teachers, inspects schools, supervises programmes, distributes textbooks, issues curricula, regulates school building standards and costs, conducts such examinations as remain within its purview, provides for the distribution of scholarships and bursaries, and maintains liaison with school trustees and with home and school organisations. In recent years there has been a trend toward decentralisation, of curriculum as in Ontario, or in responsibility for supervision, as in the larger urban centres. Again, the introduction of the larger unit of administration has reduced the load on the central office in each province.

Most of the officials in departments of education are recruited from the ranks of teachers and principals who have taught in the school system of the province, generally and predominantly in its rural areas, and because of this they tend to be both conservative and conventional with respect to educational development. Relatively few educators from urban educational systems find their way into departments of education since the salary disparities discourage them. Also, relatively few women find their way into the departments, despite a predominance of female teachers in the provincial educational systems. However there is a trend towards correcting this imbalance.

In some jurisdictions departments other than education may be responsible for some or other aspect of education. Departments of health may administer or help with the administration of health education; the department of labour may supervise apprenticeship programmes; the department of youth may look after recreational provisions; the department of agriculture may concern itself with agricultural studies and the department of the attorney general with reform schools and schools in penitentiaries.

Departments of education also have general and special curriculum committees, made up of representatives from the schools, the universities, business and industry and from labour and the community at large. These committees provide valuable advice and an insight into some of the changes taking place in the various spheres of society.

ORGANISATION

For the purposes of administration each province is divided into school districts, each governed by a school board of from five to twenty citizens elected for a period of one to three years. These school trustees have the responsibility for ensuring that the schools under their jurisdiction are administered in accordance with the provisions of the Schools Act covering such matters as attendance, length of school terms, observance of holidays, employment of personnel, school buildings, local school budget, and related matters.

In larger school districts a superintendent of education may be appointed to help the board discharge its responsibilities. Where the system is very large, as in the case of urban systems, several assistant superintendents may also be appointed. In these instances, the board, upon the advice of the superintendent, will appoint the principals and teachers in the system and arrange for their supervision. Each district superintendent is responsible for the conduct of the schools under his jurisdiction, subject to the general policies spelled out by the school board and in line with those of the department of education.

In some jurisdictions there will be one school board to administer elementary schools, a second for secondary schools, and a third to administer a variety of separate schools which may or may not be part of the regular school system. In addition, there are boards which administer community or junior colleges, and boards of governors to administer universities. From this plethora of boards it is obvious that the citizenry are involved in the administration of the school system at all levels, though all decisions are subject to the ultimate approval of the department of education; the universities, however, operate under separate Universities Acts and are autonomous in determination of policy.

FINANCE

Elementary and secondary schools are financed by taxes levied by municipal bodies against property and by provincial funds obtained from general revenue. Universities are financed by grants from provincial governments, student fees, endowment funds and subsidies from the federal government. The following table of expenditures is indicative of the order of costs involved:

Expenditures on Education from 1958 (millions of dollars)

Sources of Funds	1958–9	1969–70	1970–1	1971–2
Local government taxation	491·6	1,671·3	1,960·9	2,154·6
Provincial governments	521·9	3,717·5	4,002·3	4,483·7
Federal government	100·0	734·5	739·2	830·3
Private Sources	116·5	551·4	640·6	729·1
Total Sources of funds	1,235·0	6,674·7	7,343·0	8,197·7
Expenditures on Education				
Elementary and Secondary education				
Public	933·9	4,227·1	4,708·4	5,190·1
Private	6·7	87·4	96·1	99·5
Teacher training outside of Univ	11·7	23·2	15·9	8·9
Higher education	168·7	1,602·0	1,762·7	2,018·4
Other formal education	72·5	279·6	357·9	438·8
Total formal education	1,193·5	6,249·5	6,941·0	7,755·7
Vocational training	41·5	425·2	402·0	442·0
Total Expenditures	1,235·0	6,674·7	7,343·0	8,197·7
Per cent of Gross National Product	3·3	7·9	8·1	na

Source: *Quick Canadian Facts*, 1972–73, p 92

It is clear from this that in the period 1958–72 the overall expenditures on education, especially by the federal government, rose significantly; the increase continues, in all parts of the educational system. The need for a national and international perspective on education requires no clearer argument.

The total expenditure for all forms of education in Canada for the year 1971 was approximately \$8,000 million representing about 20 per cent of all taxes levied by federal, provincial and municipal governments.

In particular expenditures increased for the education of the handicapped, the Indians and the Eskimos, as well as for those in need of scholarships. Significant, too, is the increase for vocational and technical training and for cultural activities generally. The increased expenditures for the ancillary educational agencies such as museums and libraries suggests that the concept of education is no longer limited to schools. At the same time these expenditures indicate ways and means for the federal government to shape education despite jurisdictional limitations.

Projections indicate that by the year 1980 overall expenditures on education in Canada will approach $16,000 million. Municipal governments spend a larger percentage of their total revenues than do provincial governments, larger by some 10 per cent. Provincial governments are ready to remind us that theirs is the exclusive responsibility for education, but their expenditures do not entirely meet the changing needs of their communities. In as much as 80 per cent of the population is now resident in urban centres, the urban municipalities carry a larger share of the burden of education than their local tax base and other sources of revenue enable them to sustain in line with urban expectations and aspirations. Provincial governments have been reluctant to share their revenues with their municipalities, though willing to let them assume their responsibilities. The discrepancies between the two help to account for the difference between what is and what is possible in education. Four provinces, British Columbia, Alberta, Manitoba and Nova Scotia, use an equalisation formula in order to ensure that even the poorest tax areas receive a minimum level of education.

FEDERAL GOVERNMENT

Despite many inhibiting factors the federal government has found ways and means of making significant contributions to education. Indeed some sixty departments and agencies of government are engaged in one way or another in furthering education for a total cost of the order of $2,000 million a year. The federal contribution takes the form of programmes sponsored and developed by particular departments. The Department of

Health and Welfare, for example, initiates and sponsors health and physical education activities and has also encouraged sports and athletics. The Department of Indian Affairs and Northern Development administers the educational schedules for Indians and Eskimos. The Canadian Broadcasting Corporation helps prepare educational radio and television programmes. The Departments of Mining and Natural Resources, Trade and Commerce and others prepare brochures and booklets on various aspects of the economy for use in schools and colleges. Information Canada collects and collates information about Canada, and prepares this for publication and distribution to all public and private educational and community organisations. The Department of National Defense operates 69 schools in Canada at its military and naval establishments, accommodating some 29,000 students in 1970, and 12 schools overseas which took 6,000 students in 1971. No provincial government could make contributions of these kinds on its own, despite having sole jurisdiction for education. It appears that the definition of education assumed in 1867 has been broadening from precedent to precedent.

PROFESSIONAL ASSOCIATIONS

There are in Canada a wide variety of professional associations serving education. The Canadian Teachers' Federation serves as an umbrella organisation for the provincial teachers' associations; the Canadian Education Association, and its offshoot the Canadian Council of Ministers of Education, both in the main represent the policy-formulation and supervisory and administrative cadres of education; there are also the Home and School and Parent-Teacher associations; the Canadian School Trustees Association; the Canadian Association of University Teachers; and the Association of Universities and Colleges of Canada. In addition there are such organisations as the Association Canadienne de Développement International, the Canadian Association for Adult Education, Canadian University Service

Overseas, and the Canadian Council for International Co-operation, that serve education both at home and abroad. These, as
well as others, are essentially funded by their membership,
though some do receive governmental subventions either on a
maintenance or special project basis.

Other organisations like the Canada Council, the Social
Science Research Council of Canada, the National Science
Council and the Canadian Commission for UNESCO, are
subsidised by the federal government. The Canada Council, for
example, subsidises scholarships in the arts, letters, and humanities and supports theatres, museums, orchestras and similar
cultural bodies throughout the country. The Social Science
Research Council of Canada helps to finance research and
development projects in the humanities and the social sciences.
The National Science Council is responsible for financing pure
and applied research in and out of universities in all areas of
science. Recently the federal government appointed a Minister
of Science and Technology to further scientific and technological
research in Canada, in industry as well as in the universities.

Several provinces have cultural funds of their own to support
professional and cultural activities of local interest and extent.
Quebec has been at the forefront in this endeavour, having the
most comprehensive approach to cultural development.

One of the main problems confronting national professional
associations in Canada is that distance precludes easy and economic convening of committees for purposes of planning and con-
certed effort. The federal government has become sensitive to
this problem and now provides funds for travel to learned-
society meetings.

CANADA'S EDUCATIONAL EFFORT

In July 1972 the Canadian press released the following news
item based on studies conducted by the Organisation for
Economic Co-operation and Development:

CANADA LAGS IN EDUCATION PER CAPITA CONSUMPTION

Ottawa (CP)—Canada led all other major western countries in population growth during the 1960s, but set no records in the things that count in measuring a country's standard of living. Statistics compiled by the 23-member Organization for Economic Co-operation and Development show that the only country to exceed Canada's 1·77-per cent a year growth in population was Turkey, where the population grew by 2·5 per cent a year. Since 1970, population growth in Canada has slowed to about 1·3 per cent a year.

OECD's indicators of living standards include per capita consumption, expenditures on education as a percentage of the gross national product and the number of new houses, cars, television sets, telephones and doctors available per 1,000 population. Canada ranks at the top of the list in none of these. It does rank second to the U.S. in private consumption her head of population—$2,050 for the year 1969, compared with $2,850 in the U.S. But it ranks eighth, behind Denmark, Finland, Italy, Netherlands, Norway, Sweden and Switzerland, in the amount of its total output devoted to education. Sweden led with 7·8 per cent of GNP going into education; Canada spent 5·65 per cent.

Sweden also led in the number of new dwellings per 1,000 population, 13·7. Canada ranked fifth with 9·3 new houses and apartments per 1,000. Canada ranked second to the U.S. in the number of cars per 1,000: 311 for Canada, 426 for the U.S. Sweden ranked third with 277. The U.S. and Sweden outranked Canada in the number of television sets per 1000, population— the U.S. with 409, Sweden with 296 and Canada with 294. The same countries outranked Canada in the number of telephones per 1,000—the U.S. with 543, Sweden with 497 and Canada with 425. Canada ranked far down the list with the number of medical doctors, 1·14 per 1,000 population. Italy topped the list with 1·79 and Canada ranked 15th, leading only Finland, Ireland, Japan, Luxembourg, Portugal, Turkey and Yugoslavia.

Canada should be able to do better than rank eighth on a list of twenty-three nations in terms of expenditure on education. An expenditure of 5·65 per cent of GNP on education is a devastating indictment of a proclivity for materialism and of an inability on

c

the part of municipal, provincial and federal authorities to join forces in achieving the best educational systems possible. Certainly there is critical need for federal and provincial authorities to reconcile their respective constitutional responsibilities for education in the interests of the country as a whole.

Neither has paid sufficient attention to the fact that social, economic, scientific and technological changes in the social order require national as well as provincial education policies regardless of original jurisdictions. Hopefully both governments will sink their differences in the national interest.

3

Systems of Education

SYSTEMS

THE wide variety of schools making up the educational complex in Canada is shown in the accompanying table:

Educational Enrolment from 1958/9

Type of School or Course	1958–9	1970–1	1971–2	1972–3
Elementary and Secondary				
Public and Separate Schools	3,450,844	5,818,177	5,821,860	5,758,520
Overseas Schools	5,092	5,867	4,600	4,500
Private Schools	141,683	130,222	122,580	115,150
Indian Schools	31,353	27,556	26,780	25,940
Blind and Deaf Schools	2,340	4,066	4,075	4,100
Vocational Education				
Private Trade Schools	10,769	na	na	na
Trade Courses, apprentices	6,358	60,362	60,618	na
Vocational High Schools	81,224	na	na	na
Post-secondary Courses	5,857	122,249	145,580	169,985
Business Colleges	19,068	na	na	na
Universities and Colleges	86,500	316,690	341,030	363,900
Teacher Training:				
Teacher's Colleges	15,723	10,507	5,000	4,400
Faculties of Education	—	na	na	na

In the 1972–3 school year there are 15,424 publicly-controlled schools, employing 266,941 teachers and there are 951 private schools employing 6,351 teachers. There also are 241 Indian schools, 67 Northern Administration schools (12,000 pupils of whom 40 per cent as Eskimos and 20 per cent Indians), 11 overseas schools operated by the Department of Defence, employing respectively 241,300 and 670 teachers.

Source: *Quick Canadian Facts, 1972–73*, p 92

The approximately 6 million students attend public and private elementary and secondary schools whose educational philosophies and practices differ markedly from one part of Canada to another. Yet there are enough similarities in courses of study, textbooks and teaching practices for students living in widely different parts of Canada to recognise much in common.

The table above indicates that vocational and technical education programmes have increased in popularity and that higher education is proving attractive to a larger proportion of the population. Both of these developments reflect the fact that educational opportunities are within reach of many who formerly would never have dared aspire to an education of any kind.

These systems of education involve well over a quarter of the population in the role of student, teacher, principal, supervisor, superintendent and trustee—and even more if one includes the Home and School and Parent-Teacher associations. Despite this wide involvement of the population, however, the direction and development of education is left to the discretion of the professionals and the politicians who between them, with a nod in the direction of the trustee, shape the future of the schools.

DISTRIBUTION BY GRADES

Enrolment by Grade, Publicly-controlled Schools 1969–70

Grade	Enrolment	Grade	Enrolment
Kintergarten	358,970	Grade VIII	446,797
Grade I	499,233	Grade IX	432,695
Grade II	444,962	Grade X	392,271
Grade III	491,471	Grade XI	338,740
Grade IV	484,516	Grade XII	201,981
Grade V	477,178	Grade XIII	49,532
Grade VI	467,253	Other	153,907
Grade VII	457,711	*Total*	5,697,199

In the 1972–3 school year there are 15,424 publicly-controlled schools, employing 266,941 teachers and there are 951 private schools employing 6,351 teachers. There also are 241 Indian schools, 67 Northern Administration schools (12,000 pupils of whom 40 per cent are Eskimos and 20 per cent Indians), 11 overseas schools operated by the Department of Defence, employing respectively 241, 300, and 670 teachers.

Source: *Quick Canadian Facts, 1972–73,* p 92

The above figures for the school year 1969–70 show the Canadian school to have an average holding power of 60 per cent and while this is far from the ideal it yet represents a considerable advance over earlier periods. The drop-out rate begins to manifest itself clearly by grade 10 and accelerates markedly through to grade 13 when only a small percentage remain. In as much as grade 13 is being phased out in favour of community college entrance this figure does not represent the true situation. The holding power of schools varies considerably across the country from approximately 80 per cent in British Columbia to approximately 5 per cent in the Northwest Territories. As a result of these and related figures, changes in school schedules, differentiated curricula and a wider choice of alternatives have been introduced, and these measures have succeeded where they have been implemented. The community college as an increasingly viable and popular alternative to the university has provided another incentive for students to continue their studies through to completion of the secondary school.

PRIVATE SCHOOLS

Canada has private, fee-charging schools, ranging from the traditional boarding schools for the sons and daughters of the well-to-do, to day-schools for the children of parents who believe that more freedom in education is necessary than is found in the public sector. Boarding schools may cater for either boys or girls or both, and offer educational programmes for grades 1–12. In some instances these schools provide for the age group six to twelve, in others for ages nine to eighteen. Whatever the organisation, these private schools must adhere to the academic requirements of the province in which they are located, though no limits are set for their extra-curricular programmes which can be quite elaborate and varied. The student-staff ratio is better than that of the public school system, but then this is one of the main selling points for these schools. No public funds are available to them, and endowments are very limited except in a

few instances. The heads of most private schools belong to the
Federation of Independent Schools, which is designed to protect
the interests of its constituent members and, where necessary,
help in obtaining public support for denominationally oriented
schools.

Parents of modest means dissatisfied with the somewhat
lock-step, regimented, strictly secular climate of the public
school are turning to privately operated systems in increasing
numbers, even though the average costs per boarding student
for these schools has risen from $1,200 to $3,000 per year. Two
types of private school are, however, losing ground, the girls'
finishing schools and the schools of the religious orders. Private
schools, in order to remain viable, have had to depend upon
large financial donations which have over the years tended to
fall. Government subsidies have helped to cover some of the
losses, but by no means all.

There are also privately operated schools concerned with
preparing people for business offices, barbers' shops, hairdressing
parlours, modelling, accounting, real estate, driving, foreign
languages, art, dancing, music and computer operation. Their
scales of fees depend upon the length and level of training. Most
of these schools must be licensed to operate as educational institutions but the criteria are not too rigorous.

DENOMINATIONAL OR SEPARATE SCHOOLS

All provinces in Canada have separate or denominational schools
for a variety of religious and cultural groups including Roman
Catholics, Seventh Day Adventists, Anglicans, Chinese, Japanese,
Mennonites and Jews. Wherever possible these schools follow
the regular programme of studies of the province in which they
are located, differing only in respect of the religious and cultural
teachings which identify them. In many instances parents choose
them less because of their religious commitment than because
they wish their children to have a set of values they believe are
not cultivated in the public sector. The schools may receive

their full share of tax support, as in Ontario and Saskatchewan, no support at all, as in British Columbia, or only partial support, as in Manitoba.

These schools are administered by their own boards of education whose members are drawn mainly from their own constituency or congregation. The responsibilities of the board extend to the hiring of teachers, arranging for finances, maintaining liaison with community and department and generally passing on all decisions affecting their school or schools. By and large they have difficulty in financing their programmes, in obtaining and keeping qualified teachers and in obtaining and maintaining the learning resources essential to a quality education.

In 1969 the MacKay Commission issued a report entitled *Religion, Information and Moral Development*, which dealt with religious education in the public schools of the province of Ontario. In essence the conclusion of this report was that all religious views and value systems should be recognised by the schools. In the province of British Columbia the opinion has recently been expressed that the public schools should have a course or courses in comparative religion, enabling students to become acquainted with the value systems recognised by various peoples. This broader perspective appears to be needed.

HOME AND SCHOOL

The ties between home and school are fostered by Home and School and Parent-Teacher associations, to be found in most provinces in Canada, all affiliated with a national body. Each provincial association provides an umbrella organisation for the individual home and school groups, which vary in size, activity and influence depending upon the local support. The most effective groups are associated with elementary schools where the parents are keenly interested in the progress of their children. Home and School programmes may take the form of meetings between teachers and parents, during which the principal and his staff spell out the philosophy of the school, explain the way in which the curriculum is being implemented, or arrange for meetings between parents and teachers.

Home and School associations in secondary schools are fewer; by the time parents have seen their children through the elementary stage and attended six or seven years of Home and School meetings, many of them are no longer disposed to continue the exercise. Again, principals and teachers in secondary schools are not all convinced that parental presence is appreciated by their progeny and hence give little or no support. On the other hand there are Home and School associations that help secondary schools with equipment, books and projects which they might not otherwise be able to have.

The associations meet several times during the school year to discuss school programmes, school-community relations, or special projects, but they have never really been given financial support or encouragement to exercise their educational concerns. Nor have school trustees fully appreciated the value of active Home and School associations in promoting the general welfare of education. Rather there has been a competitive tension among departments of education, teachers, trustees and parents, not always to the advantage of the children or students.

EDUCATION OVERSEAS

The Canadian government, through its Canadian International Development Agency and in co-operation with teachers associations and departments of education, sends teachers and educational specialists of various kinds to developing countries to assist them in improving their educational systems. In 1969 Canada had 767 educators and 232 advisors serving in some 29 developing countries. At the same time 1,870 students from developing countries were in Canada, under Canada's sponsorship, studying agriculture, teacher training, natural-resource development, business administration, medicine, engineering and other subjects. Canadian University Service Overseas is a voluntary agency, supported in part by federal funds, which places university students, faculty and community members in countries around the world in need of specialists—ranging from accountants to vocational education instructors. These volunteers must be prepared to serve the host government for a period of two years, and have gone to such areas as Jamaica, India, East Africa, Nigeria, Peru and Colombia. Other overseas educational aid programmes are arranged by provincial governments, universities or churches, independent of though co-ordinated with federal efforts. Thus the Manitoba government arranged educational assistance for Thailand, the Quebec government for several French-speaking countries, while the University of British Columbia helped the University of Singapore in the development of its economics department.

The universities and colleges of Canada enrol some 9,000 overseas students in their graduate study courses covering the spectrum of academic and professional disciplines. A few of these students remain in Canada, but many return to their native lands to make available the skills they have acquired. Canadian experience has suggested that there may be an advantage in sending teams abroad to overseas colleges and universities, so that students could acquire their expertise without having to make a radical adjustment to a new system and approach to education.

Another dimension of Canada's educational efforts abroad is to be found in the Canadian International Development Agency's executive service overseas. This provides for executives from business and industry on leave from their firms to place their expertise at the disposal of countries in need of it. As one president of a corporation who returned from a satisfying service overseas experience said:

A fifth of the world lives in affluence compared with the four-fifths that have nothing. The gross national product per capita in Canada is about $3,000. In four-fifths of the world it is a $100 or less. Canadians are in a good position to serve in developing nations. Nobody bears any resentment against us. We were never a colonial power. They don't suspect us of wanting to exploit them under the guise of giving aid. Since Canada was once a colony, Canadians have an understanding how colonial people are. Being a bilingual nation helps. Many developing nations speak French as a second language—West Africa, North Africa, Laos, and others.

> John Bene, 'Wildwood of Canada, CDA', as quoted
> by Charles Wolverton in *Province* (12 February 1970)

But Canada's contributions to the social, economic, technological and educational development of other countries, while significant in terms of both dollars and the expertise of students, teachers, professionals of many kinds and businessmen, have not been, and are not, adequate to meeting the real needs. Canada's schools have not yet brought to the fore the international component of social studies and other aspects of the curriculum in a form and manner sufficient to make a lasting impression upon its future citizens.

MUSEUMS AND GALLERIES

There has been a considerable expansion in both the formal and informal education opportunities in the arts in Canada. On the formal side, the study of the arts has been encouraged not only by the schools but by colleges and universities. On the less formal side, public art galleries and museums provide Saturday classes, conduct tours for school pupils and adults, radio talks, lectures and concerts. Most major cities in Canada, as well as many smaller ones, have galleries and museums and all make their services available to school as well as community.

SCHOOL AND COMMUNITY LIBRARIES

Although a national library was not established in Canada until 1953, there has been a long tradition of having good libraries in urban schools and communities—though not always in rural areas. Departments of education make special grants to schools for the purchase of books and media materials. In some instances community libraries are established convenient to schools while many schools open their own libraries to communities. School libraries are broadening into curriculum resource centres, with tapes and records as part of their collections. It has been estimated that government, university, school and public and special libraries stock something like 75 million books, periodicals and pamphlets.

SOCIAL TRENDS

Developments within Canada's educational systems need to be seen in the context of changing social trends. One social scheme in particular has been of special value to the children of Canada. Under the provisions of the Family Allowance Act of 1944, monthly allowances are paid for all Canadian children under sixteen, one of the conditions attached being that the child must comply with provincial school-attendance regulations. Among other benefits these allowances have helped greatly in equalising educational opportunities. A second scheme introduced by the federal government in 1964 provides monthly non-taxable allowances to help young people of sixteen and seventeen with defraying school costs. The provinces of Newfoundland and Quebec have their own somewhat similar schemes.

Since World War II the people of Canada have had health services on a much broader base than hitherto; an orbital space station ensures television reception as far north as the Arctic; the benefits of science have been made available to the below-average earner by way of housing, foods and clothing; technological advances in medical services, food preparation and delivery, transportation and communication, computerisation and the like have eased and lengthened the life of large numbers of the population; and there has emerged a new and deeper appreciation of the benefits to be derived from the wide variety of cultures within Canada.

All these trends may be found reflected in various parts of the educational system in the form of new equipment and new courses of study, new resources with which to enrich some of the earlier courses in the schools, new departments of government and new divisions in departments of education. Changing patterns of education are to be found in both private and public systems and at every level. Although these changes have captured the imagination of public and professional bodies alike with innovations in television broadcasting, computerised timetables and modular schedules, there has nevertheless been a growing concern with moral education. School administration is moving from an authoritarian to a humanitarian approach, and to an adoption of methodologies allowing for a better balance between individual and group activities.

4
Elementary Education

THE BEGINNING YEARS

OVER 4 million children are enrolled in public and private elementary schools in Canada, which range from kindergarten to grade 8 (in several systems to grade 6 or 7).

School sizes vary but, in the main, in urban areas there will be approximately 500–600 pupils of both sexes with about 20 teachers including the male or female principal. The trend has been towards smaller schools, to afford pupils and teachers more opportunities for getting to know one another as persons. In rural areas there are still one-, two-, or three-room schools where the teacher or teachers are responsible for a combination of grades which may reach from grade 1 through to grade 12, the majority of pupils usually being in the elementary grades.

Elementary-school buildings range all the way from the simple wooden structure of a one-room rural school to the most modern and architecturally sophisticated designs incorporating open areas, curriculum-resource centres, cafeterias, and gymnasium and play areas. The sense of well-being created by these buildings and their carpeted classrooms contributes significantly to the quality of the learning situation established. The quality of building is, nevertheless, no substitute for the quality of instruction which must always remain paramount. Most urban, and certainly all rural, elementary schools are situated in spacious playgrounds which afford ample opportunity for free and formal play for the children. Many schools, too, have play parks as an integral part of their school playgrounds or use one belonging to a nearby community club.

Generally elementary schools come well-equipped with instructional technology. Most schools have radios, film and slide projectors, teaching machines, and the best have film loops and open- and closed-circuit television. Some of the schools, particularly those with open areas, have enough film loop and slide projectors as well as science equipment to enable several groups of students to work with these at the same time. Blackboards, greenboards and tackboards still constitute the basic media of communication largely because these provide for the greatest degree of flexibility and creativity in teaching.

In the larger urban elementary schools the principal is the senior administrative officer who is responsible to the board, through the superintendent. In smaller school districts the principal is responsible directly to the local school board. The teachers in their turn are also responsible to the board but report directly to the principal of their particular school. Each school and its complement of teachers is afforded the expertise of various supervisors, as well as given formal inspection either by a department of education official or by a delegate of the super-intendent.

Most teachers of elementary grades assume responsibility for the teaching of the language arts, social studies, reading and arithmetic in their particular classes and, when necessary, call upon specialists for the teaching of art, music and physical education. In some areas, these specialist teachers are made available to several schools and travel from school to school as necessary. With the increase in the number of teacher aides or ancillaries available, more and more elementary teachers are able to give more individual attention to their pupils. Nevertheless, there has been a significant increase in the number of schools and systems providing counselling services and the use of various 'test batteries' to identify the talents and capacities of the individual child. In recent years, too, more attention has been given to the value of field trips, elementary teachers taking their classes to discover the way of life in the local post office, factory or airport.

THE DAILY SCHEDULE

The daily schedule of the elementary school generally begins at 9 am and concludes at 3.30 or 4 pm with an hour or an hour-and-a-half break at noon and a recess period of fifteen minutes in both morning and afternoon. In the primary and elementary grades, class periods are of ten to twenty minutes, and in the upper elementary grades twenty to forty minutes, these period lengths being based upon the assessed attention span of the children. Schedules may be altered by either school board or principal to suit season or occasion, for example in some rural areas or during exceptionally inclement weather. Some schools arrange the timetable to allow the teacher to have her class for the entire school day, while others allow this for only morning or afternoon sessions so that children may benefit from contact with other teachers for various subjects. In general, though schedules are laid out for the year, there is a greater tendency to let the teacher use the time according to the needs of the programme of studies and the students.

The school year is divided into two parts, from September to December, and from January to June. A seven to ten day holiday is allowed at Christmas and New Year, with approximately a week's break at Easter. July and August are holiday months. In recent years school districts have begun to provide remedial and special-education classes for a few weeks during either July or August for those children who have for one reason or another failed to achieve their goals.

Some school districts in rural areas still arrange their school year to allow for planting in the spring and harvesting in the autumn, a practice quite prevalent at one time but becoming rare with a decreasing agricultural community. Northern areas still have to adjust their school year to accommodate the native peoples' hunting seasons, when entire families, including school-age children, are involved. Since some northern schools bring their children in by plane at the beginning of the term, adjustments have to be made here too, to suit the weather and the different communities that lie along the Arctic Ocean.

PRE-SCHOOL PROVISIONS

Canada has day-care centres, nursery schools and kindergartens, designed to provide the pre-school child of two to five with the educational circumstances suited to his needs. Most pre-schools, particularly day-care centres and nursery schools, are privately operated and financed, though public systems are beginning to develop the nursery sectors. Kindergartens are to be found in most urban systems, though here again the private sector still dominates, but there are some in rural areas. The children have opportunities for singing, playing games, dancing and drawing, all designed to bring about improvement in co-ordination, associating with other children and developing independence. The kindergarten programme is designed to augment the child's experiences in the home and/or the nursery school and also to provide him with more formal learning situations than he has had heretofore: he is given formal opportunities to develop oral and written language skills, to relate easily and freely with other children in group activities, and to develop a positive attitude towards school.

Pre-school classrooms generally have no more than twenty to twenty-five children, with the result that each child is able to receive individual attention, particularly since many nursery schools and kindergartens make use of teacher aides or assistants to help the regular teacher. These pre-school programmes, too, provide for the involvement of parents at various periods of the school year, thus easing the transfer of the child from the protected atmosphere of the home to the wider social world of the school, where the process of socialisation proceeds more rapidly.

Parents of very young children are concerned for their offspring and eager to participate in the work of school and to help the teachers.

Kindergarten and nursery-school children usually attend school for half days only, though in some instances the day extends from about 9 am to 3 pm.

PRIMARY GRADES

The primary grades 1, 2 and 3 of the elementary school are generally devoted to developing the basic skills of reading, writing and arithmetic. The language arts play a significantly important part at this stage, with attention given to both oral and written skills including lettering. As far as arithmetic is concerned the child is given a wide variety of experiences to help him grasp the quantitative character of the world around him. In addition there are social studies, nature study, art and music. Considerable attention is paid to games, play, physical education and dancing, all designed to continue the socialisation process begun earlier as well as help the total social, emotional, physical, and intellectual maturation of the child. A good deal of time is spent on the development of oral communication skills and by the time a child has completed this stage of his schooling he is expected to have made the social and emotional adjustments necessary for obtaining fullest benefit from the next stage.

INTERMEDIATE GRADES

In grades 4, 5 and 6, children pursue a more extensive course of studies. Reading and the language arts give way to literature, composition and grammar. Arithmetic extends beyond counting to reach for mathematical concepts, with a view to laying a sound basis for fundamental numeracy and further study. Understanding of the local community gives way to social-studies concepts, including those of history and geography, and field trips into the local community begin to be important. In addition general science takes the place of nature study, and

D

students are encouraged to discover the real world for themselves and report their findings to their classes. Music, art, and physical education continue to have their place, and arts and crafts increase in importance, as do vocational classes including wood-work and homecraft. So the intermediate-grade pupil is expected to perfect his basic study skills, acquire the knowledge essential to a measure of independent study, and be able to work alone or with others.

MIDDLE SCHOOL

The middle school is designed to meet the needs of students of eleven to fourteen, in grades 6–8. The programme of studies and activities aims at individualising instruction, integrating studies, and providing for flexibility and efficiency of operation; it allows for a good measure of self-planning so far as the student is concerned, and for continuous progress, as well as for open access to media and materials. In some respects the middle school represents an upward extension of the open-area school generally associated with the early elementary grades and is essentially experimental.

GROUPING

The thirty to forty children of the typical elementary school class will usually be arranged in three or four groups of ten or more, for purposes of instruction. This grouping may be based upon general intelligence as measured by intelligence tests, reading skills, language ability, peer-group interests, numeracy, or on a combination of these depending upon the particular purpose of the instructional group. Some schools group children homo-geneously or heterogeneously at the beginning of the year, using four or five criteria, and allocate them to classes on these bases. Others follow a purely heterogeneous scheme and leave the teacher free to arrange her own groups. Open-area schools have the most flexible arrangements, allowing children to move or be moved from group to group, depending upon the particular interests or skills involved. In several instances the child's age or social maturity determines the group to which he is allocated.

REPORT CARDS AND PROMOTION

All schools are required to provide the home with a report of the child's performance in school. These report cards range in style from a single numerical figure indicating how many marks out of a hundred the student obtained on each subject to elaborate anecdotal reports describing his personality characteristics, relations with teachers and fellow students and general and specific attitudes towards his studies. Report cards constitute a perennial basis for debate among members of the teaching profession and quite often also for Home and School associations. Whatever form these cards take they are usually sent to the home three or four times a year, and parents are required to acknowledge their receipt. Some schools provide opportunities for parents to meet the teacher or teachers, either at school or at home, to discuss matters arising from the report. Students in these as in other elementary grades must achieve an average of 50 per cent in all subjects in order to be promoted to the next grade. Exceptions are allowed in special circumstances.

INNOVATION

Several schools have adopted the continuous-progress method of moving children through the various stages or levels of their studies; the idea is that each child proceeds at his own pace and receives such individual attention as is indicated and possible. The system provides for maximum adaptation of the course of study to the needs of the individual child.

Team teaching is another approach to instruction which is gaining popularity, particularly in open-area schools. Ontario and British Columbia have moved furthest with this, although the method is also to be found in western Canada and in a few places in Quebec and in the Atlantic Provinces.

Teacher aides, or assistant teachers, are increasingly used in some of the systems, on either a paid or voluntary basis. These aides are in many instances married women in the school community, with or without teaching experience, willing to devote a few hours a day for two or three or more days a week to helping the regular teacher; there are regular and in-service courses designed to prepare them.

Programmed instruction has begun to make its way into elementary schools though primarily at the upper level. Essentially experimental at this stage, its potential for relieving the teacher of much routine instruction is recognised, as well as the fact that the independence of the student as learner is reinforced. There are as yet not too many programmes suitable for all subjects in the elementary schools. Their scope is limited and the cost is high, but these matters will probably be rectified in time.

The out-of-doors school to be found in Ontario, British Columbia, Saskatchewan and elsewhere is designed to afford urban children an opportunity to study their regular school subjects in a wilderness area specially set aside for this purpose. In addition to developing an appreciation of the great outdoors and the forces of nature, students are able to live for a period of a week or more with their classmates and teachers and get to know them as fellow human beings. Mathematics, social studies, language, literature, and particularly science, are studied in relationship to the natural setting.

Considerable attention has been given to modifying the elementary-school curriculum in line with the findings of research into the behaviour of the child and with the increase in knowledge about man and nature. The new mathematics has been introduced throughout the elementary school, with debatable results. The teaching of reading is given constant attention and so is the nature and character of the reading material, which has met harsh criticism because of its paucity of challenging ideas and the limited scope it offers for understanding the community at large. The methodology of instruction in the elementary school has been under review, and less lecture and more independent study is being advocated.

Review of present methodology has also brought forward the idea that students be given more responsibility for planning, initiating and conducting their own strategies of enquiry, and more opportunity for widening the use of non-print materials, as well as for following out-of-school courses that contribute to their studies and their understanding. Perhaps one of the more important changes is the recognition that emotionalism has an important place alongside intellectualism in shaping the individual as a participating member of society.

OPEN-AREA SCHOOLS

Many of the new elementary schools built in Canada in recent years have open areas large enough to accommodate 50–200 children. The open-area concept eliminates rigidities and inflexibilities, as well as walls, and creates learning situations which allow for emotional as well as intellectual development. The child in the open area has the benefit of a team of teachers, and the advantage of a wide array of resources which he can use as freely in informal situations as in formal. The learning situations are so arranged as to make it possible for students to move from one section to another according to needs. The open-area concept, too, provides for the continuous progress of the student who may proceed from level to level in his subject at his own rate, and so from grade to grade. The wider age-range to be found in open areas also provides a more real-life setting for the individual. The open-area system also makes it possible for students and teachers to work together in learning situations that are considerably more informal than those in regular classrooms. In consequence, communication between student and teacher is improved, barriers between disciplines are broken down and incidental learning increased. Thus the open area has made possible more flexible arrangements for study for both children and teachers: children are given the use of a wider range of audio and visual aids, increased opportunities for frequent handling of scientific and technical equipment and more co-operative learning activites. On the other hand, some students and teachers prefer smaller groups and quieter surroundings, the disciplined situation of the regular classroom and the more formal approach to study it offers. In part, these caveats on the open area derive from a lag in the design of specially suitable curricula and in the inclusion of the open-area concept in teacher-training programmes. It should be recognised, too, that old patterns of study prevail despite new surroundings and new circumstances. Another disadvantage is that children may find it difficult to adjust when they move to the closed system of the junior or senior secondary school.

SPECIAL EDUCATION

Children suffering from social, emotional, physical or intellectual disabilities are given special attention in separate classes or special schools or, where the degree of impairment is not very serious, in regular classes. The blind, the deaf, the spastic, the autistic, the multiple-handicapped and others are provided with the facilities and training to help them acquire the skills necessary to becoming independent members of society. To this end class sizes are limited to between ten and fifteen, and in some cases may be as low as five, or even one.

There have been a number of surveys and studies directed to discovering the nature and extent of the need for special education in Canada, and the results have pointed to a great gap in educational provisions. A *National Study of Canadian Children with Emotional and Learning Disorders* (entitled for short *One Million Children*), sponsored by a consortium of educational organisations including the Canadian Association for the Mentally Retarded, the Canadian Council on Children and Youth, the Canadian Education Association and the Canadian Mental Health Association, and edited by David Kendall and Karaline Ballance, found that approximately 12 per cent of

Canadian children suffered from one or more disabilities that required special attention. The report of the Ontario Committee of the Commission on *Emotional and Learning Disorders in Children* substantiated the parent-study findings. Still another study, *The Standards for Educators of Exceptional Children*, underscored the importance attached to giving these physically, emotionally and mentally deprived children the attention their condition deserves.

The following survey conducted by the Canadian National Institute for the Blind in 1968 points out how numerous are the children who require special attention:

	BC	Alberta	Man	Sask	Ont	Que	Mari-time
School-aged blind	212	172	119	77	512	548	207
In school schools for blind and day schools (total)	156	92	74	77	373	499	141
Institutions for retarded includes hospital, day school and special classes	33	34	34		139		
Multi-handicapped at home	15	6	9		51		
Residential school for retarded	22	21	15		31		

These figures only include those legally blind children who have come to the attention of the CNIB. They do not include Indian children living on reserves or partially seeing children.

Cited by Dr Sally Rogow, 'Blind Retarded Children in Canada', in *Special Education in Canada*, vol 46, no 3 (March–April 1972,)

It should be noted that despite a long tradition of special education facilities for the handicapped in Europe and in Asia, Canadian departments of education were exceedingly slow in assuming responsibility for the education of disabled children, and it was only when parents, doctors, and teachers co-ordinated their efforts that support was forthcoming. The aforementioned reports are evidence that a new era has dawned. The development of the British Columbia Mental Retardation Institute, directed by Dr Charlotte David, has made it possible for teachers, doctors, nurses, social workers and others to co-ordinate their services on behalf of these children. This team approach is proving very effective in the rehabilitation of the handicapped.

DISCIPLINE

Discipline in the elementary school is left to the individual teacher to administer on the understanding that corporal punishment, if found necessary, must be administered in the presence of a witness, and then only after the most serious infractions against the social good. Most teachers use persuasion, admonishment and removal of privileges before resorting to physical correction. 'Strapping' of children is frowned on, and though still found in some systems, the idea of outlawing it—as was done in British Columbia in 1973—is gaining ground. There are, of course, various schools of thought on the best way to cultivate discipline, ranging from the ultra-rigid to the ultra-flexible, depending upon the particular psychology involved. However, for the most part, teachers in Canada are firm in their discipline in school with a view to cultivating self-discipline in the child and producing ultimately the responsible citizen in society.

5
Secondary Education

THE SECONDARY SCHOOL

SECONDARY schools range in size from the single secondary classroom in rural areas, where one teacher gives instruction in all subjects to grades 9–12, to the larger urban high school accommodating 2,000–3,000 students. The rural secondary student is obviously at a disadvantage, since the options open to him are limited to those the one teacher can offer in the brief time available to him. Town and city secondary schools on the other hand afford their students a wide variety of courses and specialist teachers. The larger secondary schools too are able to offer the expensively equipped vocational and technical courses of study which are beyond the means of small schools with limited staff.

The secondary-school day begins at 9 am and concludes at 4 pm. Club activities and extra-curricular activities including sports and games may continue until about 6 pm. Most school programmes are organised on the basis of four or five 40–50 minute periods a week in each subject, with three or four periods of instruction in the morning and two or three in the afternoon. This pattern of timetable has been modified in some schools to the module system which provides for 10–20 minute periods throughout the day. In this system there is considerably more flexibility in that various combinations, ie 40, 60 or 80 minute periods, are possible. The secondary-school year is generally the same as the elementary year.

ADMINISTRATION

Each junior or secondary school is administered by a principal together with one, or more than one, assistant principal. The principal is responsible to the school board through the superintendent, and may also be assisted by one or more supervisors of instruction, who travel from school to school offering assistance to teachers in their work as well as serving as consultants and advisors to the principal. Teachers are involved to varying degrees in administration, either by way of committees or through meetings convened by the principal on a weekly or monthly basis. There is also a trend towards administrative committees of teachers who serve the principal in an advisory capacity. This attempt at the democratisation of the school has met with approval wherever it has been introduced. In some instances students have also been given places on the administrative committee with good results.

The principal's responsibility for the operation of the school includes maintenance of the buildings, the administration of the curriculum, utilisation of staff, dealing with parents and community organisations, reporting to the superintendent and the board, consulting with supervisors and adjudicating staff and student problems. Each principal perceives his task in the light of the type of school and community in which it is located. In an economically and socially deprived area he has to try to conduct the school programme in a way that helps to compensate for these deprivations. Schools located in districts where a variety of cultures obtain require the principal and his staff to take the various value systems in the community into account when dealing with students and their parents.

The principal and his staff have the assistance of clerical personnel to help maintain the essential records, reports and correspondence, but rarely enough of them, so that teachers have to spend time and effort on record-keeping that could be done at less cost by others. The practice of employing aides has helped here to some extent.

JUNIOR SECONDARY SCHOOL

The junior secondary school, comprising grades 7, 8 and 9, or grades 8, 9 and 10 in some systems, is designed to provide the student with an opportunity to explore the various areas of study open to him in the sciences, the social sciences, the humanities and the technologies and to discover the suitability of his talents for these. So students who enter the junior secondary school are given a wide range of choices and are permitted to transfer more or less freely from one section to another. They are encouraged to postpone a final choice of subjects until they are more or less sure what avenue they wish to follow. There are approximately a million and a half children in these grades in Canada, the schools ranging in size from about 500–1,000 students. In some instances these grades form the senior section in an elementary school; in others they constitute the junior division of a senior secondary school.

Because students in the junior secondary schools are engaged in exploring their own potentialities, guidance and counselling services play an important part. All students are given intelligence tests (though these are being reduced because of doubt of their value), psychological tests and vocational-interest inventories, as well as achievement tests, and on the resulting assessments the school advises the student on the right choice of courses. The curricula provide for extensive visits to industrial, commercial and community organisations.

THE SENIOR SECONDARY SCHOOL

Senior secondary schools are variously organised to accommodate students from grades 9–13, in one or other combination of grade patterns. Some secondary schools have grades 10–12, others 9–11. In each instance the completion of the work of the secondary school enables the student to proceed to a community college, a university or a technical or technological institute.

The secondary school is seen as enabling the student who has acquired the fundamental skills in the elementary school to increase his knowledge and further develop his skills, in line with his developing interest and abilities. The holding power of these schools has been increasing over the years so that students entering the senior secondary school have tended more and more to continue their studies through to graduation. There are approximately a million students in these grades throughout Canada.

VOCATIONAL-TECHNICAL

Secondary vocational and technical schools cover a wide variety of course offerings in preparation for a wide variety of trades: building construction, commercial training, domestic service, machine shop, radio and television servicing, electrical construction, welding and so forth. Some technical schools offer more advanced training leading to auto-body repair, beauty culture, carpentry, cabinet-making, refrigeration and air-conditioning, and the like. These vocational and technical education programmes are in most instances guided by representatives from labour and industry who sit on department of education committees responsible for supervising the training.

Students may enrol in vocational-education programmes for periods of study ranging from three weeks to three years, several of which have apprenticeship arrangements. The following table indicates that ample opportunities are available. Students may, if they wish, proceed from these studies to technical and technological institutes, or take employment and there undertake further study on a part-time basis. However, apprenticeship arrangements are too few at present and a far better system for this is needed.

SCHEDULING

A variety of schedules are used to organise secondary school

Full-Time Enrolment in Vocational Courses, School Year 1968–9

Course	Nfld	PEI	NS	NB	Que	Ont
Publicly Sponsored						
Vocational high schools	—	921	2,150	10,553	—	231,763
Post-secondary technical courses	713	—	913	467	14,010	27,004
Apprenticeship courses	978	87	2,231	225	—	10,122
Trade schools and vocational centres	5,521	1,494	10,142	8,078	—	71,784
Training in business and industry			354	—		14,849
Diploma schools of nursing	649	186	953	978	6,728	9,460
Nursing assistant schools	460	31	265	152	717	2,250
Privately Operated						
Trade school courses	—	—	298[1]	291	—	3,182
Business school courses	—	—	582[2]	571	—	2,615

Course	Man	Sask	Alberta	BC	YT and NWT	Canada
Publicly Sponsored						
Vocational high schools	7,935	4,735	19,648	22,763	554	—
Post-secondary technical courses	1,224	1,145	6,420	3,265	—	55,161
Apprenticeship courses	1,222	2,121	7,946	3,432	38	28,402[3]
Trade schools and vocational centres	7,846	5,494	6,400	17,196	435	134,390[3]
Training in business and industry		1,826	4,478	1,291	59	
Diploma schools of nursing	1,246	1,164	2,114	1,622		25,100
Nursing assistant schools	283	198	605	450		5,411
Privately Operated						
Trade school courses	414	361	851	1,457		6,854[3]
Business school courses	1,209	1,096	726	911		7,710[3]

[1] Includes one school in Newfoundland. [2] Includes one school in Newfoundland and one in Prince Edward Island. [3] Excludes Quebec.

Source: *Canada Year Book* (1970–1)

programmes. The traditional schedule provides for five to seven periods a day, for five days a week. In some systems students move from room to room, while in others the teachers do so.

Modular scheduling, noted in an earlier context, provides for periods of 10–20 minutes which can be arranged in any combination, thus making for greater flexibility and easier accommodation of both curricular and extra-curricular offerings. Modular scheduling, too, has the advantage of allowing students to pursue out-of-school activities related to their academic interests, and to engage in part-time industrial and commercial enterprises as part of their education and training. The ungraded secondary school allows students to proceed through the programme of studies at their own rates and because of this classes and individual study periods are arranged in a combination of traditional and modular plans. In some schools block schedules are used which permit a student to study algebra, history or science for periods extending through an entire morning or afternoon and for one complete semester. The adoption of the semester system indicated more flexible scheduling, and this has been adopted by a few secondary systems.

CURRICULA

Students in secondary schools may pursue courses made up of various combinations of subjects subsumed under the broad divisions of the social sciences, the physical sciences, the humanities and the vocational-technical fields. Those seeking to prepare themselves for the university and ultimately for the professions are encouraged to pursue a combination of studies from a list of courses including language, history, mathematics, geography, economics, biology, chemistry, physics, art, music and the like. Students who opt for the trades or the services choose from commercial, industrial, and other specialised areas. Opportunities are also available to study commercial subjects, such as typing, book-keeping, accounting, office management and subjects in the industrial world—construction, drafting, mechanics, electricity, electronics and so forth. These studies are pursued not only in the regular day schools but in evening schools and in special short courses.

School curricula, and especially secondary-school curricula, have come under public scrutiny to an increasing extent. Members of the business community have questioned the necessity for prolonged study in some areas of the school programme (eg some aspects of literature, history and art), querying the practical relevance of these studies, recommending more on-the-job training better suited to the needs of the business world.

> Since the beginning of the century, it has been abundantly evident that the applicant with the most schooling has been given preference by employers. But it is equally evident that formal education is not the be-all and end-all of a successful career in business.
>
> A lack of formal education does not mean a man lacks an inquiring mind or the necessary intellect to reach the top. Nor is it true that business holds a man's formal education in higher esteem than it holds the man himself.
>
> Ralph N. Roger, 'Prolonged Study Years "Alienating" Our Youth?' *The Financial Post* (17 February 1968)

Business is not alone in its criticism of the school. Many students find the disparity between the perspectives of school and those of society causes them to question the credibility of the school and its curriculum. Recent studies of the content of Canadian textbooks have revealed that Canadian children are being presented with prejudiced views regarding national, religious and minority groups. In particular, social-studies textbooks dealt badly with the Canadian Indian, the treatment of the Japanese during World War II, Nazi responsibility for the holocaust, civil rights and the entire question of race and minority relations. Dr Garnet McDiarmid and Dr David Pratt, in a study sponsored by the Ontario Human Rights Commission, stated among other things:

Indians came off very badly and in 95 per cent of illustrations
were depicted half-naked or clothed in historical or tribal dress.
They were also shown as being primitive, aggressive and hostile.
Africans were generally shown partly naked and aggressive and
subordinate to white. Both Africans and Asians were pictured
doing only manual labor.

The teaching of French, too, has come under scrutiny since
bilingualism and biculturalism became a national issue. Much
more emphasis is being placed on learning to speak the language
and to begin learning early, continuing through the secondary
school to the university. Unfortunately, not all educational and
political authorities are prepared to recognise the civilising values
of the appreciation of a variety of cultures. The following report
of an interview is indicative of such an attitude:

> Education Minister Donald Brothers says the provincial govern-
> ment doesn't plan to improve French-language instruction in
> B.C. schools with its $700,000 federal grant.
> Instead, he said in an interview, the money will be used to pay
> for French programs as they now exist in the schools.
> The grant is B.C.'s share of a federal government incentive plan
> to extend bilingual educational opportunities in all provinces.
> Ottawa is making available about $50 million to the provinces for
> the 1970–71 school year.
>
> Marian Bruce, 'Grant Won't Upgrade Instruction
> in French', *The Vancouver Sun* (19 February 1971)

In sharp contrast the teachers of British Columbia took another
stand:

> B.C. School teachers have overwhelmingly endorsed use of French
> in schools where a French-speaking majority warrants it.
> Nearly 1,000 delegates to the B.C. Teachers' Federation annual
> convention here almost unanimously endorsed the Comox resolu-
> tion. Less than twenty were opposed.
>
> Wilf Bennett, 'Teachers Support French', *The Province*
> (18 April 1968)

In 1973, the teachers of the province were supported in their stand on the teaching of French when the newly elected government announced through its Minister of Education, Eileen Dailly, that $750,000 in federal grants for French-language school programmes would be made available to school boards. Again in contrast, 5 per cent of elementary and secondary education in the province of Prince Edward Island is conducted in French, while French is taught as a second language in all other secondary schools.

Educational television, radios and teaching machines have made it possible to enrich and lend variety to the curricula and their presentation. In addition, departments of education have given teachers more freedom and responsibility for adjusting curricula to the needs of their students. The former practice of having teachers restricted to courses of study and textbooks prescribed by the department of education has been considerably relaxed. The curriculum, too, has benefited by having work experience in industry or business related to or integrated with school studies. In this way students are given the opportunity to apply their learning in real-life situations; those following courses in commerce and carpentry, for example, profit greatly from arrangements of this sort.

Secondary-school curricula have also been expanded to provide for driving, drug and alcohol education. Sex education, too, finds its way into most secondary studies, while beauty and physical culture are included in health and physical-education programmes.

EXTRA-CURRICULUM

The extra-curriculum of the secondary school is considered 'extra' only in the sense that it is conducted outside the regular school day. It is made up of a variety of clubs, including photography, stamp, chess, art, journalism, dancing, games, history, poetry, travel, all designed to afford interested students opportunities to get together with others of like interest, increase their

E

knowledge and perfect their skills. Each club in a school is sponsored and supervised by a teacher but in the main is operated by the students themselves, who also raise such funds as are necessary, though schools attempt to subsidise some of the operations. Wherever possible the activities of the club are related to the regular curriculum so that they reinforce what goes on in school hours.

Where schools are located close to clubs maintained by the community, some of the extra-curricular activities are integrated with those of the club, students and teachers working with the director of the club in order to avoid unnecessary duplication. Since community clubs operate during the evening and during the weekends as well, this arrangement has the effect of extending the extra-curriculum of the school.

EVALUATION

The evaluation of student performance in secondary schools has been undergoing changes in recent years. The traditional three-hour examinations at the end of the term in each subject have given way to more frequent assessment of student achievement over the course of the year. Whereas a student used to be promoted to the next grade only if he passed in all his subjects, a system of subject promotion now allows him to avoid repetition of subjects in which he has achieved a pass grade. Grading is based generally on 100 points, 50 per cent constituting a pass and 80 per cent or over constituting an honours performance. Where a letter-grade system is used, A is honours, B and C are passes, and D and E are failures, with option of repeating the examination if a D is obtained; an E would require the student to repeat the course. In addition to tests and examinations, student performance is assessed on the basis of potential as measured by intelligence tests, the results of which may be used in conjunction with the record of academic achievement. As in the case of the elementary schools, report cards are issued by the school for the parents about three or four times a year. Again, school visits are arranged for parents to give them an opportunity to discuss these, and teachers and counsellors make it a practice to discuss reports with both students and parents.

COUNSELLING AND GUIDANCE

The counselling and guidance department of secondary schools provide both students and teachers with information valuable to the personal, social, academic and vocational development of the student. Though each classroom teacher does assume some responsibility for the academic and personal guidance of the student, it is the counsellor who, with the results from a wide variety of tests and instruments for measuring aptitudes and abilities, is able to provide student, parent and teacher with objective evidence useful in arriving at a decision regarding the student's future course of action. In addition, the counsellors are able to bring together a great deal of information bearing upon vocational opportunities which is useful to students in deciding upon their career. Both federal and provincial governments, as well as some industries, provide literature and statistics to help students to their decisions. As far as the vocational and technical schools are concerned, government manpower offices, established to assist men and women to employment, send personnel to these schools before graduation time to assist graduates to suitable positions in business and industry.

CORRESPONDENCE COURSES

For those students living in remote parts of Canada where there are few if any secondary schools, departments of education provide correspondence courses in academic and commercial subjects leading to a high-school certificate. The teachers employed by the departments prepare course outlines and study guides, and each student is required to complete the set exercises, mailing them to his or her teacher in the department. Teachers do give careful attention to their students and provide copious notes as a guide for them. Where students are located sufficiently

close to a high school they are encouraged to seek the assistance
of the teachers there. Students enrolled in correspondence courses
take the regular provincial examinations in as many subjects as
they wish in any one year.

STUDENT GOVERNMENT

Student government plays an important part in the conduct of
the affairs of the secondary school. Each class names or elects a
student to a student council, which is responsible for supervising
student social and extra-curricular activities and for giving such
assistance to the principal and his staff as is necessary from time
to time. In most instances the decisions of the council are subject
to veto by the principal, but this is used only on rare occasions.
These student councils often publish a school newspaper,
conduct fund-raising activities for school projects and assist in
maintaining discipline through establishing codes of conduct.
Among the more important reasons for supporting student-
council activities is that they give students a sense of responsibility for the conduct of their own affairs as well as an appreciation of the democratic process. It is these councils which quite
often serve as liaison between the school and the community,
and help explain the role of the school in society. Experience has
indicated that the quality of student attracted to serving on the
council is high and that generally these students are able to provide excellent leadership in the school as well as maintain an
excellent scholastic record.

Student councils have in many instances appointed 'ombuds-
men' to ensure fair treatment of students by staff and other
students. This has proved successful and is being adopted widely.
These councils, too, have on occasion undertaken assessment of
school programmes and made recommendations for improvement.
They have also visited municipal and provincial governments
with a view to seeing how democracy works but have not always
been inspired by the level or manner of debate engaged in by
the politicians.

STUDENT ATTITUDES

The Canadian secondary-school student is in general no longer the passive individual he once was. Students of both sexes are not prepared to accept the social shibboleths of the day. One counsellor, on reporting student attitudes, said:

> . . . many of the complex problems confronting today's urban society stem from the conflicting polarization of attitudes adopted on one side by youth seeking revolutionary changes and their elders of the establishment striving to maintain the status quo. They (the students) are protesting the hypocrisy of parents who profess to support racial equality, but who react violently when their children date those of another religion or color, the hypocrisy of teachers who pretend to support democracy while operating rigidly authoritative classrooms, the hypocrisy of principals who set up toy governments from whom they accept suggestions on minor projects while continuing to run the school to suit the staff.
>
> Dr Sheila Thompson, 'Students Oppose Hypocrisy',
> *The Vancouver Sun* (13 March 1969)

Certainly Canadian students are critical of the traditional and ultra-conservative approaches of teachers and principals in the conduct of school affairs: by virtue of the wide knowledge they gain from the media, the paperback and their travels, they are in a much better position than ever before to appraise the adequacy and relevance of the programmes offered them. Also healthier living conditions, better food and advances in medical techniques have contributed to the earlier maturation of the student, who is consequently a more alert and aggressive individual. This is the student who considers the worst evils of man's education to be the development of anti-humanistic and essentially technocratic attitudes, who believes that there is a serious credibility gap between what the school professes and what society confesses, who feels that his initiative and imagination is drained away by rigid regulations and requirements.

6

Post-Secondary Education

HIGHER EDUCATION

HIGHER education in Canada, sometimes referred to as post-secondary education, includes a wide variety of institutions, ranging from degree-granting universities, of which there are about 55, the 23 degree-granting theological colleges, junior and community colleges and colleges of advanced technology of which there are about 150, and another 175 private and public colleges and continuing education centres of various kinds. In the school year 1969–70 there was an estimated total of 481,500 students enrolled in one or other forms of higher education, of which 300,000 were in university programmes and 181,500 in non-university courses.

Since World War II there has been a dramatic increase in the number of young people and adults who have either continued their studies to higher education or have returned to studies earlier interrupted. During the past two decades there has been an over 400 per cent increase in students attending higher educational institutions: from approximately 80,000 to over 450,000. The increase in expenditure for higher education has been of a comparable order, indicative of the importance attached to the education of the individual and of the place of higher education in the nation. When the total expenditure of the country approaches 10 per cent of GNP, and expenditure on higher education constitutes a large portion of the increase, then it can be seen that there has been a radical change in the assessment of the role of education in the development of the country and its peoples.

The rapid increase in enrolment in higher educational institutions and in the costs of maintaining these led inevitably to studies seeking assessment of their role. The New Brunswick Higher Education Commission, the Commission on Relations between Universities and Governments in Canada, the Study of Higher Education in British Columbia, and the reports of the Economic Council of Canada are but a few of the studies undertaken for this purpose and to recommend plans for development. For the most part these studies envisaged the growing importance of higher education, the need to recognise the place of associated institutions such as the community colleges and the institutes of technology, and the need of the federal government to retain its interest and support of higher educational institutions.

Because the costs of higher education have been increasing by leaps and bounds, some provincial governments have been seeking to exercise more control over university budgets. However, the principle of university autonomy is still generally respected, and universities in those provinces where an attempt at closer control has been made have been able to resist successfully. Nevertheless, the message of governments to universities has been made clear: uninhibited expenditures in pursuit of unrealistic and uneconomic ideals can no longer be tolerated by governments responsible for maintaining a reasonable balance among all the services required by society. The universities for their part are conscious that they are no longer the sole avenue to higher education, that indeed the institutes of technology and the colleges of technology provide an education more suited to many students and to industry and commerce, and that in consequence universities need to reassess their value to society as a whole. There are already indications that students, parents, and businessmen are alert to these new perspectives.

GOVERNMENT OF UNIVERSITIES

The original universities in Canada were established by French and English religious groups in Nova Scotia, New Brunswick, Quebec, Ontario and at a later date in Manitoba, Saskatchewan and Alberta. Provincial public universities as distinct from the aforementioned denominational institutions were established in Manitoba, Saskatchewan, Alberta, Newfoundland and more recently in Quebec by their respective provincial legislatures. The religious colleges at first limited their enrolments to students from within their own denominational groups but over time these restrictions gave way to the ecumenical movement and to the wisdom of being eligible for federal grants.

All universities function under the aegis of a Provincial University Act which provides for the administration of universities and stipulates the terms of reference for each higher educational institution. Authority for the administration of a university is vested in a board of governors elected and appointed by alumni (graduates of the university) and by the provincial government from members of the general population who express an interest in university affairs and who have the time and capacity for them. Essentially, therefore, this cadre of people is drawn from the business and professional community and there have been remarkably few people from labour represented on university boards. It may well be that if university boards are to reflect the views of the industrial community some correction will have to take place.

The internal government of universities is by a heirarchy that includes a chancellor elected by the alumni for a period of three years, a vice-chancellor or president who is appointed by the board of governors, is responsible to it and holds office at its pleasure, one or more vice-presidents who serve as assistants, a registrar to maintain the records, and a bursar to look after financial affairs. The faculties and schools of the university are headed by deans and directors appointed by the president for unspecified terms. Recently there has developed a trend to appoint or elect heads of departments, directors, and deans for specified terms to permit rotation of office. Ultimate responsibility for the conduct of academic affairs resides in a senate that is made up of representatives from the academic staff, the community at large, the alumni, and representatives from various professional associations. In the past several years students have been appearing on university senates, and in a few instances even on boards of governors, to the advantage of all concerned.

Members of staff are appointed generally for probational periods of from one to three years, as lecturers, assistant professors, associate professors or full professors, with tenured appointment depending upon their performance during the early period.

Several provincial governments have departments of university affairs which help co-ordinate and supervise their particular complex of universities without infringing what has been traditionally accepted as the institution's autonomy on its academic affairs. In the province of British Columbia, an academic board helps the government distribute the federal and provincial funds made available to the universities. In Ontario a provincial committee of university presidents, as well as other higher-education committees, advise the province's department of university affairs and its universities.

All colleges and universities in Canada are members of the Association of Universities and Colleges of Canada, which serves as a forum where its members can discuss matters of common concern. The Canadian Association of University Teachers provides a similar forum for members of faculty not part of the administrative structure.

ADMISSION

The student who wishes to attend a university has to have a secondary-school certificate testifying that he has satisfactorily completed eleven or twelve years of schooling and is therefore eligible for the first year of university. If he or she completes a

thirteenth year in a secondary system he is then eligible to enter
the second year of the university. Since the advent of the
community-college system (see p 79), grade 13 is being phased
out. Graduates of the academic stream of community colleges
may transfer to the third year of the university, providing the
curricula of the particular sections of the two institutions are
adequately articulated. Those students who wish to pursue a
career calling for vocational or technical training may go from
secondary school to a vocational school, to the technical section
of a community college or to an institute of technology.

There has been a tendency in recent years to relax some of
the rigorous regulations governing admission and procedure to
and within the university, somewhat along the lines of the open-
university concept. Certainly there appears to be an increase in
flexibility and it is now possible for students to pursue their
academic and professional objectives by way of transfer of credit
between and among universities, travel seminars, interdisciplinary
programmes of study and research, home-study arrangements,
educational television credits and the like. The fact that students,
both graduate and undergraduate, are being involved in the
planning of these changes in university curricula is further testi-
mony that these institutions are paying heed to the needs of the
emergent future.

STRUCTURE

The typical college and university in Canada has a faculty of arts
for students of the humanities and social sciences, a faculty of
science, and one or more professional schools. The larger
universities, such as McGill, Montreal, Toronto and British
Columbia, have several professional schools including engineering, medicine, law, social work, librarianship and teaching.
Smaller institutions, such as York, Victoria, Simon Fraser,
Laval, Calgary or Lethbridge, have one or two of these schools,
established with a view to meeting local or national as well as
international needs, but all dependent for their success upon the

fiscal and human resources available to them. Arts and science studies leading to a Bachelor of Arts or Science degree may be three or four years in length. Professional school programmes range from two to five or more years, depending upon the nature and character of the degree or diploma sought.

The traditional structure of the university, however, is being challenged by students, faculty and public. Some consider that the university, as presently organised and administered, is hopelessly outdated. Others see it as incapable of preparing students adequately for the real world. Still others view the hierarchies and bureaucracies of universities as stultifying to imagination and initiative for both faculty and students, benefiting only those who are prepared to play the power and personality game on the road to preferment. With all these and related views being expressed, students consider alternatives, including the establishment of 'free universities' as at Rochdale in Ontario, and in Vancouver, British Columbia. These institutions, however, are not viable since the resources necessary to maintain them are not readily available.

UNIVERSITY STUDENTS

University students in Canada more often than not work during the summer and sometimes during the year to earn their fees. These fees may range from $400 to $800 a year depending upon the faculty and course load. In addition, if the student elects to live in a university residence he will have upwards of $100 a month to pay during the seven or eight months of the university year. If the university is on a trimester system the student's costs may mount accordingly. In general the university year runs from September through to April with holiday periods at Christmas, Easter and during the summer break.

The life of the university student is enriched by a wide variety of clubs designed to afford him associations and activities complementing his studies and interests: international study groups, political science clubs, skiing and skating, music, art and painting, debating and other clubs of similar character. Students in residence are better able to take advantage of these than is the day or commuting student. Most universities now have overseas tours, many arranged by the students themselves.

The usual university schedule, beginning around 7 am and lasting until the dinner hour at about 6 pm, allows ample time for library and laboratory work but it also allows for students getting together over coffee or beer to discuss the lectures of the hour or the political issues of the day, to engage persons or ideas or both in a continuing exchange.

Students have recently begun to use their extra hours to move into the community at large with special services to those in need. These services take a variety of forms. In one case students go to schools to help children with learning difficulties in any subject area. In another, law students operate a free legal-aid service, and social-work students find opportunities to help the needy. In many other ways the university student does seem to appreciate his privilege in benefiting from higher education and seeks opportunities to help those less fortunate than himself.

DROP-OUTS

According to *Statistics Canada*, a survey of undergraduate student withdrawals from Canadian universities for the years 1969–70, 1970–1 and 1971–2 clearly revealed that the 'optimism of the sixties has . . . been replaced by a certain hesitancy on the part of young Canadians'. The results of the survey varied across the country, the largest drop-out taking place in British Columbia (20 per cent plus) and the next largest in the Prairies (15 per cent); 10 per cent was the figure for the Atlantic Provinces, 5 per cent for Ontario and approximately $2\frac{1}{2}$ per cent for Quebec. While there are a variety of reasons for these undergraduate drop-outs from higher education, there is no doubt that the arguments advanced for continuing education have been eroded by the high unemployment rates for graduates and by the general climate of uncertainty which encompasses social, economic and political developments throughout the world as well as in Canada.

FINANCE

The universities and colleges of Canada receive approximately 70 per cent of their operating funds from federal and provincial governments, 20 per cent from fees, about 1·4 per cent from endowments and 8·6 per cent from other sources. These figures vary from private to public institutions but generally reflect the current situation.

The following table of income and expenditures for universities and colleges is indicative of the order of sums involved:

Current Income and Expenditure of Universities and Colleges, Academic Years 1959–68

Academic Year Ended	Current Income					Total Current Expenditure
	Endowments & Investments	Government Grants	Student Fees	Misc	Total	
	$'000	$'000	$'000	$'000	$'000	$'000
1959	4,668	74,294	33,546	11,373	123,881	124,564
1960	5,082	87,863	40,789	14,132	147,866	148,659
1961	5,332	115,524	45,991	14,396	181,243	181,311
1962	7,834	121,461	56,249	25,062	210,606	211,330
1963	8,191	142,606	62,397	27,107	240,301	244,015
1964	10,308	168,626	75,573	28,785	283,292	289,931
1965	7,986	200,412	89,738	44,632	342,768	345,222
1966	9,030	256,915	110,624	49,780	426,349	432,332
1967	9,506	384,521	129,953	57,604	581,584	579,215
1968	10,228	521,084	144,490	64,780	740,582	738,510

Source: *Canada Year Book* (1970–1)

The magnitude of the increase between 1959 and 1968 is highly significant in terms of the increase in demand as well as in costs. Another aspect that calls for attention is the increase in student fees. As every increase has the effect of discouraging the economically deprived, there is a tendency for equality of educational opportunity to go out of the window. And even though federal and provincial governments increase the availability of scholarships and bursaries, there is nevertheless a net loss to the poorer student.

Although education is acknowledged to be constitutionally a provincial responsibility, the federal government has had to step in and provide funds to the extent of approximately 50 per cent of the costs of post-secondary education. In 1969–70 the federal contribution to education by way of direct transfer of funds amounted to $620 million. This was spent on vocational training, adult occupational training and research grants to universities. In addition, approximately $67 million were made available to enable students to borrow up to $1,000 annually, interest-free for five years, to pursue their higher education studies. More recently legislation has been brought in enabling parents to deduct up to $50 per month from taxable income for each child attending an institution of higher education.

Another avenue of federal aid was introduced in 1966, when the Health Resources Fund Act provided some $500 million to enable schools, hospitals and other institutions to develop and equip health-training facilities. This was followed by provincial governments establishing their own funds, either health or athletic, in order to retain some measure of autonomy in this realm.

Canada's provincial governments generally require their universities to submit estimates of budget, following which negotiations take place as to what constitutes a reasonable grant that university and government can live with for the ensuing year. Grants are not yet made for more than one year at a time.

Although direct federal assistance to education increased markedly in the past decade it also increased indirectly through the support of health, welfare, culture and recreation. During the same period federal expenditures in health and welfare increased from $1,824 million to $3,653 million, while expenditures on culture and recreation increased from $169 million to $324 million.

In particular, federal assistance to post-secondary education has taken the form of payment to provinces for costs of universities, community colleges and the like, student-loan programmes, and bilingualism development. The projections for the immediate future in these areas is for expenditures reaching $667 million. If one were to broaden the definition for education and include expenditures for culture and recreation then another $368 million will be spent in the 1972–3 period.

COMMUNITY COLLEGES

The most important development in the field of higher education has been the emergence of junior or community colleges. These two-year institutions have generally three streams, one academic, one technical and the third devoted to further education for adults. Admission to the first two streams is on the basis of high-school credentials, but if a student has none they may be achieved through the third stream. These colleges have succeeded in attracting many students who feel that the university is either economically or academically beyond them, or who prefer to attend institutions closer to home. Ontario, British Columbia, Alberta, Manitoba and Quebec have moved furthest in developing them and attracting large numbers of students. Community colleges are administered by their own boards, either appointed or elected, and are financed by fees and subventions from the public purse obtained through taxes. Enrolment varies from 1,000 to 5,000 students, depending upon location and variety of courses of study. In Quebec, these institutions are known as *collèges d'enseignement général et professionel* (colleges of general and vocational education); in Ontario they are colleges of arts and technology; and elsewhere colleges of one title or another, all offering the essential trinity of avenues: academic, technical and continuing education. The reception which has been accorded these community colleges across the country attests their popularity.

The community college appeals to students on several counts. In the first instance tuition costs are below those of the university; second, the central focus of the institution is teaching, so that students have a better chance for individual attention; third, there are a number of institutions scattered throughout any one province so enabling students to live at home while attending college; fourth, since there are three avenues open to the student he has a chance to explore them before making a final choice; fifth, they offer a shorter and more direct route to an occupation than is provided by the university. The student who leaves high school and chooses the academic avenue in a community college, in preference to one at a university, can still proceed to the university after he has ascertained his own interests and abilities. As far as continuing education is concerned, the community college offers students of advanced years opportunities suited to their particular interests and abilities in the form of schedules and hours of instruction that suit their convenience. In brief, the community college represents a stage of education intermediate between the high school and the university, meeting the needs of many students who require a longer exploratory period than is otherwise possible.

CONTINUING EDUCATION

In addition to the continuing-education programmes conducted by departments of education and by universities, both federal and provincial employment and manpower agencies have been funding and developing retraining courses for men and women who have either lost their jobs or been trained for occupations that are oversupplied with personnel. These are financed jointly by provincial and federal authorities and by industry; they may be on or off the job depending upon the type of industry, the kind of training, and the number of students involved. Several industries move on from on-the-job retraining to regularising apprenticeship training for young people and adults. Another pattern is to be found at the Quetico Centre on the shores of Eva Lake in north-western Ontario. Here a variety of educational opportunities is provided for young men to handle heavy construction, play folk music, be self-sustaining in woodland areas, develop skills in a wide variety of vocational-training plans—

ranging from carpentry to managing tourist lodges—including those required for the disabled worker.

The Alberta Petroleum Industry Training Centre is an example of a special type of school designed particularly for those intending to work within the oil industry. The school has proved attractive to students from around the world. Another form of continuing education is represented by the Frontier College, a unique institution which reflects the pioneering spirit still evident in Canadian education. This college, started in 1900 by A. Fitzpatrick and E. W. Bradwin, employs university students to work alongside men labouring in the forests, the mines and the construction industry. In the evening and at weekends these students teach their fellow labourers fundamentals in language, mathematics, civic, history, literature and economics, to mention only a few of the wide-ranging interests of these groups. The system is supported by government, industry and the donations of individuals.

The Department of Citizenship and Immigration helps to finance and conduct classes for newly arrived immigrants, at which they acquire language skills and a knowledge of the laws and customs of the country as well as of its history and development. These classes are offered under the auspices of both urban and rural school systems and are almost completely subsidised by the federal government. This citizenship education may be extended to include social evenings, cooking classes, debates, discussions, theatre groups, poetry reading, all with a view to enabling the participants to learn to apply their newly acquired skills in the new social setting.

TEACHER EDUCATION

Canadian teachers are prepared for their profession in teachers' colleges administered by departments of education or in schools or faculties of education administered by a university. Teacher-college courses are generally one or two years in length and lead to qualifications for an elementary teacher's certificate. Schools

F

and faculties of education offer courses of study of one to five
years, leading to either elementary or secondary school teaching
certificates. In both instances, colleges and universities are
responsible for the academic and professional preparation of
teachers but certification remains the prerogative of the provincial
government department of education.

One-year teacher-college students attend two terms, September to December and January to June, in the course of which they
study the philosophy and psychology of education, administration,
methodology in one or more school subjects, library services,
and in some instances religious studies, and are required to
demonstrate professional competence in school practice. Where
a student is enrolled in a two-year programme his studies are
pursued in these areas to a greater breadth and depth, and lead
to interim certificates good for up to five years, after which the
teacher has to engage in further professional and academic studies.

Teacher-preparation programmes in universities take essentially two forms. In the first, students complete a first degree in
arts, science or related field, and then enter a one-year course of
studies in pedagogy, leading to a Bachelor of Education degree.
In the second instance, students holding a secondary-school
certificate with an average of 60 per cent or better, may engage
in a set of studies integrating arts, science and education and
proceed to specialise in teaching at the elementary, secondary,
and in some instances adult level. The degree granted at the
conclusion of these studies is that of Bachelor of Education. The
courses of study available to students in these professional
schools include history, philosophy and sociology of education,
educational psychology, tests and measurements, librarianship,
music, art and physical education, counselling and guidance,
programmed instruction, audio-visual education, computer-
assisted instruction, inter-cultural education and technical
education, as well as the subject-matter disciplines taught in the
regular school.

In addition, prospective and practising teachers may proceed to postgraduate studies leading to a Master of Arts degree in Education or a Master of Education degree and to Doctor of Education or Doctor of Philosophy degrees. These advanced studies permit teachers to specialise in the areas of their particular interest: eg in administration, curriculum development, school counselling, educational psychology, sociology, philosophy, history or comparative and international education, mathematics and science education, education of the retarded, music, art and physical education. These graduate studies may be pursued during the regular university year, but because many teachers, principals and supervisors interested in further professional study can do it only on a part-time basis, many enrol in evening or summer sessions conducted by the universities. Nevertheless many students attend full time and complete their advanced training in this way.

In 1968-9 (*Canada Year Book*, 1971) there were 56 teacher-training colleges in Canada, 32 faculties of education in universities, and 2 institutes of technology for the training of vocational and technical instructors. Students enrolled in these institutions numbered 49,698. Most of the teacher-training colleges or normal schools, as some are still called are in due course to be affiliated, associated or integrated with university faculties, thus moving towards the day when all Canadian teachers are prepared in universities. The total teaching force in Canadian public elementary and secondary schools is about 254,000 with an additional 12,000 in private schools. In Canada 23 per cent of elementary teachers and 71 per cent of secondary teachers have degrees. Teacher aides and kindergarten teachers are trained both in community colleges and teacher-training institutions, the latter predominating in the case of kindergarten personnel.

The teaching force in Canada is sustained not only by graduates from the colleges and universities but by teachers who migrate to Canada from Britain, Australia and the United States. More recently the current has reversed and surplus teachers from Canada are seeking and obtaining positions in these countries.

In addition an increasing number of teachers are offering their services to underdeveloped countries as well as taking exchange teaching posts within the developed systems.

The status of the teaching profession has been improving as a result not only of the upgrading of the initial training as it comes under university supervision but because teachers have continued their professional studies in in-service courses within school systems and in summer sessions at universities. During the past decade the number of teachers in Canada increased by 67 per cent from 152,000 to 254,000, while the Canadian population increased by only 18 per cent. During the same period the average salaries of elementary and secondary teachers increased from $4,200 per year to $8,000. These figures represent a growing awareness of the importance of education by both the governments and the public and an appreciation of the value of teaching to society. The profession has proved attractive to many more aspirants because of an increase in the number of assistants or aides made available to the teacher, and in the number of supporting services and resources made available to the school. Again, the democratisation of school administration which now gives teachers a role in shaping policy, a place in leadership, a share in the determination of direction and innovation, and the respect due to independence of performance, has added to the stature of the teacher and the profession.

Nevertheless teachers do not enjoy the autonomy to be found in other professions such as law, medicine and engineering. Although educated and trained in colleges and universities they are certificated by departments of education and subject to the whims of whatever political viewpoints happen to be in office at the time. They have very little say, if any, as to the number of students they may teach or the amount of money they can spend on materials and books for their students. It is for these and related reasons that teachers in some instances have explored the merits of joining unions and aligning themselves with labour. For the present the professional ideal holds the balance.

UNIVERSITY GRADUATES

University and College Graduates, Academic Years 1960–1 and 1969–70

Bachelor Degrees	1960–1	1969–70	Bachelor Degrees	1960–1	1969–70
Agriculture	311	531	Physiotherapy	118	92
Architecture	84	352	Optometry	28	57
Arts	7,614	26,436	Pharmacy	281	404
Pure Science	1,614	6,699	Phys Education	245	837
Chiropractice	28	48	Social Work	245	68
Commerce	1,110	2,910	Theology	859	729
Dentistry	179	341	Veterinary Sc	56	117
Education	2,430	11,244	Others	68	205
Engineering	2,412	3,550	*Total*	20,240	60,453
Fine Arts	11	160			
Forestry	115	185	*Masters Degrees*		
Home Economics	270	568	Arts	1,408	5,768
Interior Design	9	35	Science	672	2,656
Journalism	25	37	Licence*	367	—
Law	697	1,502	*Total*	2,447	8,424
Library science	199	395			
Medicine	842	1,105	Doctorates (Earned)	305	—
Music	88	334	Doctorates (Hon)	265	1,375
Nursing	302	1,245			

* In the French language universities, Licence is the next degree in advance of Bachelor. In 1971–2, there were granted 67,600 bachelor degrees, 11,510 master and licence degrees, 1,790 earned doctorates. Estimates for 1972–3: 71,700, 12,380, 2,030.

Enrolment and Academic Staff in Universities and Colleges in Canada 1972–3

Province	Schools	Staff	Under-graduates	Graduates	Total
Newfoundland	1	615	7,550	450	8,000
Prince Edward Island	1	140	2,050	—	2,050
Nova Scotia	10	1,370	17,040	1,360	18,400
New Brunswick	4	955	12,160	740	12,900
Quebec	20	5,890	57,200	8,800	66,000
Ontario	37	10,910	128,000	16,000	144,000
Manitoba	8	1,510	18,100	1,500	19,600
Saskatchewan	12	1,330	15,260	790	16,050
Alberta	6	2,430	33,000	3,600	36,600
British Columbia	7	2,445	35,800	4,500	40,300
Canada	106	27,595	326,160	37,740	363,900

The above includes all universities and colleges offering one or more years of degree credit work beyond the most advanced high-school grade in the province in which they are located. Part-time enrolment not included above: 205,940 undergraduates, 17,860 graduates.

Source: *Quick Canadian Facts, 1972–3* p 93

The table above shows that universities have been graduating an increasing number of people who can take their place in the country's economy. Yet it is also evident that the proportion of all university graduates going on to higher degrees remains at a relatively low level considering the requirements of the country as a whole. Certainly Canada could increase its productivity in this realm, and rely less on imports to man its educational and cultural institutions. Nevertheless there is evidence that the 'brain glut' has replaced the 'brain drain' so far as the ability of the economy to absorb graduates is concerned. By 1970 enrolment in graduate studies had reached 40,141 of whom 27,966 were in full-time residence. In the same year the National Research Council pointed out that whereas in 1968 there were 80 Canadian science PhDs available for jobs and 75 were placed, by 1970 there were 160 PhDs for 90 jobs and by 1972, 240 for 85 jobs. The problem, however, is not a matter of overproduction of graduate students but rather that of the distribution of graduates to where they can best serve, whether at home or abroad.

MIGRATION OF GRADUATES

The aforementioned observations may be placed in the perspective of the following table entitled 'Story of a National Tragedy', which appeared in *The Province*, 3 August 1962. It shows that between 1950 and 1960, 43,803 of Canada's most highly educated people left for work in the United States representing a significant loss of expensively-trained manpower.

Emigration to the US of Canadian engineers, scientists and other professional persons who have moved to the US

	11-year total	1960	1950
Architects	288	33	12
Engineers			
Aeronautical	437	30	—
Chemical	439	49	37
Civil	586	75	39
Electrical	952	128	40

	11-year total	*1960*	*1950*
Industrial	199	19	4
Mechanical	1,144	86	95
Metallurgical	132	15	8
Mining	109	13	8
Engineers (Misc)	3,876	466	—
Scientists			
Agriculturalists	81	6	—
Biologists	111	13	—
Chemists	1,037	107	57
Foresters and Conservationists	92	18	
Geologists and Geophysicists	166	27	—
Mathematicians	39	7	—
Physicists	235	34	—
Miscellaneous Natural Scientists	60	2	—
Educators			
College Presidents and Deans	44	—	—
Professors and Instructors	563	65	63
Teachers	3,956	503	251
Health Services			
Physicians and Surgeons	2,124	262	260
Dentists	134	13	29
Nurses, Professional	12,407	1,365	791
Nurses, Student Professional	327	55	—
Chiropractors	34	4	4
Optometrists	32	3	2
Osteopaths	6	—	—
Pharmacists	206	18	13
Dieticians and Nutritionists	305	28	—
Veterinarians	200	9	14
Clergymen	1,659	141	170
Economists	74	14	—
Lawyers and Judges	166	18	12
Librarians	307	35	25
Psychologists	92	17	—
Statisticians and Actuaries	72	11	—
Accountants and Auditors	2,283	322	—
Designers and Draughtsmen	2,880	294	102
Farm and Home Management Advisors	24	2	4
Personnel and Labour Relations Workers	58	5	—

| | *11-year* | | |
	total	*1960*	*1950*
Social and Welfare Workers	559	56	53
Miscellaneous Social Scientists	23	—	—
Surveyors	145	25	7
Technicians			
Technicians, Medical and Dental	777	116	—
Technicians, Testing	340	49	—
Technicians (Misc)	1,556	339	—
Other Professional, Technical and			
Kindred Workers	2,037	298	129
TOTAL	43,803	5,195	2,415

Source: US Department of Immigration

Despite the recognition in 1960 that Canada stood to lose a great many graduates by 1972 it became evident that the lesson had not been learned. As indicated by a review of the Department of Manpower and Immigration report, edited by Dr Sylvia Ostry, in 1972:

> Preliminary results of a department survey of 735 national employers asking how many graduates they hired from the class of '72 show a continuing decline from last year's depressed level.
>
> The best that can be said is that the rate of decrease in job opportunities is flattening out: last year's hirings of Arts graduates declined 37% over 1970 figures; this year, 38% fewer were hired than last year.
>
> Hirings of science graduates showed a 38% year-to-year decrease, vs a 41% decrease last year.
>
> Commerce and business graduates did better: hirings this year were 2·5% up over last year, vs a 14% decline in 1971.
>
> *The Financial Post,* 'Job Market for University Graduates Declines—Again' (23 September 1972)

The prediction by Dr Max von Zor-Muehlen of the Economic Council, in the same article, of 'severe underutilisation' of two-thirds of Canadian PhDs appears to be coming true; this suggests that there is a long-overdue need for some agency in Canada to begin studying the relationship between the requirements of the economy and the productivity of its educational institutions. Although each individual must be able to choose to pursue his or her genius in vocation or profession, this can be coupled with data helpful to the individual who plans studies in preparation for a career.

HIGHER EDUCATION RECRUITMENT

Canada has need of highly trained personnel for its academic institutions. Unfortunately, federal and provincial politicians ignored population projections for higher education about a decade ago, with the result that rapidly rising enrolments in higher educational institutions necessitated the recruitment of academics from outside Canada. In particular an influx of United States educators, supported by a two-year tax suspension, upset the balance of personnel in such sensitive areas as education, the social sciences, humanities and the law. Again the politician's short-term plans prejudiced the rational development of personnel policies in higher education. This has been a matter of controversy for over a decade and promises to present continuing problems. Robin Mathews and James Steele, leading advocates of the Canadianisation of Canadian education, have been vociferous on this question. The public and the universities too have become conscious and concerned, so that corrective measures are now being adopted.

In September 1970 Arnold Edinborough observed:

If we are to have a Canadian nation, we have to see to it that the seeds of a vibrant, definite, yet not chauvinistic nationalism are sown in school, nurtured at university and rewarded in the commercial world afterward.
But as the Canadian Council of Teachers in English concluded, it's difficult to see how it is to be done when:
There are few good materials available to help teach Canadian literature and the Canadian scene because of the colonial curricula established by antediluvian departments of education.

The universities are either totally unaware of the problem or maintain a phony internationalism to facilitate the request for U.S. research funds.
The faculties of education are staffed with American researchers, often using U.S. models and plugged into U.S. computer programs.

The Financial Post (12 September 1970)

In March 1971 Dr W. R. Carruthers, President of the University of Calgary in Alberta, reported that less than half of the academic staff at that institution were Canadians, the distribution actually being: Canadians, 405; Americans 196; British 149; Indians and Pakistani 33; other nationalities 34. A national symposium on Canadian universities in May 1971 passed a resolution calling on federal and provincial governments to limit the number of foreign nationals teaching at Canadian universities and colleges. The same resolution called for legislation limiting the number of foreign nationals on the teaching staff of any post-secondary institution to 15 per cent of the total staff.

While educators and government officials debate the pros and cons of the principle of universality as it applies to Canada's colleges and universities—a principle recognised more in the breach than in the observance everywhere—the Canadian public has become concerned with this question as it affects their young people, most of whom have come more and more to appreciate Canada's own value systems and cultures.

RESEARCH

Universities also maintain a variety of research institutes concerned with oceanography, international relations, ecology, economics or nuclear studies, depending upon their particular constellation of human and financial resources. These research centres are supported by monies obtained from three sources: university budgets, foundations (of which there are many in the United States but few in Canada), and federal funds distributed by the National Science Council, the Canada Council and the

Social Science Research Council. There are, in addition, on or near to university campuses, federal research centres concerned with fisheries, agriculture and forestry, all of whose personnel are in close liaison with their counterparts in the university. The graduate divisions of the universities emphasise their research function and in many instances select problems which are critical to the development of the community and of industry and commerce. The appointment by the federal government of a Minister of Science and the establishment of the Science Council of Canada, designed to co-ordinate scientific research and to stimulate more research within the industrial community, indicates that there is an increased awareness of the importance of both pure and applied research in the development of the society.

The establishment of research councils in several of the provinces has helped to co-ordinate and stimulate research in business, industry and education. Thus the Nova Scotia Research Foundations, the New Brunswick Research and Productivity Council, the Research Council of Alberta and the British Columbia Research Council carry on research and scientific inquiry into the development and use of natural resources, as well as into a variety of social, economic and technological problems. All these councils make it possible for students to participate in their research activities on either a formal or informal basis.

7
Reform of Education

ROYAL COMMISSIONS

THE road to major educational reform in Canada is by way of the findings of royal or ordinary commissions or committees established to study a particular aspect of the educational system when it is out of phase with either society or other parts of the system. Reforms, too, are to be found going on regularly in the classrooms of the nation's schools by way of innovation initiated by the teachers, as well as by changes in policy and practice initiated by governments and school administrators. Despite the fact that education is the exclusive jurisdiction of provincial governments, and particularly their departments of education, there is sufficient flexibility within the more progressive educational systems to permit experimentation with courses and programmes by teachers and systems.

Home and School and Parent-Teacher associations, teachers' organisations and many other public bodies play their part in bringing about changes in education. The contribution to educational reform made by the public media, the press, radio, and television, cannot be underestimated since these agencies help to cross-fertilise educational systems by reporting inventions and innovations introduced both at home and abroad.

The recommendations brought in by commissions frequently lead to considerable controversy and debate before all or part of the reports are implemented. Thus in Alberta the royal commission (1972) chaired by Dr Walter Worth and charged with studying the future of elementary, secondary and post-secondary education in the province has proposed the establishment of an academy to provide a bridge between high school and university, the elimination of grade 12 college-entrance examinations, abolition of permanent certification of teachers, and alteration of the school holiday patterns to provide for more frequent breaks in the school year. Several of these constitute issues and have led to debate. In Ontario an eleven-man commission was appointed under Dr D. T. Wright, chairman of the Ontario Committee on University Affairs, to study the needs of post-secondary education in respect of student preferences, courses, institutions and finance. In Newfoundland the Department of Education was reorganised along functional rather than denominational lines, on the recommendation of the Warren Royal Commission on Education (1967–8), such proposals for change are dependent upon the governments concerned for implementation wholly or in part.

In 1973 the government of British Columbia, in the person of the Minister of Education, Mrs Eileen Dailly, appointed John Brener to head two commissions, the first to examine elementary and secondary education, the second post-secondary. These commissions are to determine to what extent problems in education are caused by the existing system, to discover if changing the system would eliminate these problems and to discover if the amount of energy spent in the present system is paying off.

The recommendations of the Royal Commission on Education and Youth (1960) initiated significant changes in Quebec's educational systems by providing for more emphasis on language instruction, for democratisation of the schools and for easier accessibility to them. The introduction of 33 *collèges d'enseignement général et professionel* (CEGEPs), a system of kindergarten for five-year-olds, the development of a University of Quebec, and the substitution of 230 school commissions for 1,714 educational boards helped modernise the system.

NATIONAL ORGANISATIONS AND REFORM

In addition to these provincial commissions there are national organisations such as the Canadian Teachers' Federation and the Canadian School Trustees Association which appoint their own committees to study particular educational problems. The Canadian School Trustees Association study of educational finance in Canada (1955) provided an important assessment of this area of education. In another case, the Commission on Relations between Universities and Governments in Canada (1970), headed by Reni Hurtubise and Donald C. Rowat, was jointly sponsored by the Association of Universities and Colleges of Canada, the Canadian Association of University Teachers, the Canadian Union of Students and the Union générale des Etudiants de Quebec. This commission recommended among other measures that the federal government transfer tax credits to the provinces, and let these bodies finance universities and colleges; also that a national commission on higher education should be established with a view to greater involvement of the public in this realm of education. Both recommendations led to considerable debate.

The survey of education (1971) in the Northwest Territories, conducted by members of the teaching and administrative staffs of that school system, contains forward-looking recommendations for the development of education in the area. These include a pre-school in every settlement, classroom assistants, all-year elementary schools, the provision of lunches, a recommended rather than prescribed list of textbooks, greater recognition of local value systems, elementary schools open to parents and more general teachers as opposed to specialists. An earlier decision to have Indian and Eskimo children begin their school studies in their native languages had proved worth while and was to be continued. A distinct feature of this report is the recognition that education in the Northland can only succeed if the school takes account of the cultural fabric of society and arranges its programmes and practices to accommodate it. The study is characterised, too, by a concern for the placement of the school product in the work force of the community and for the provision of the necessary vocational, technical and continuing education.

Reforms in education have also been influenced by studies initiated by the Economic Council of Canada, which council, though essentially concerned with the economy of the country, found it necessary to include a section or chapter on education and its bearing on the productivity of the work force. The federal government's Royal Commission on Bilingualism and Biculturalism (1967–70) also influenced educational practices in the country by bringing in strong recommendations for the more widespread use of French in government, education and the media. This report also led to a proposal for the establishment of a French-language teachers' college for the Western Provinces and for placing more emphasis upon teaching languages such as Cree, Ukrainian and German. In the Atlantic Provinces the Atlantic Institute of Education was established to facilitate co-operation in teacher education particularly at graduate level.

CURRICULAR REFORM

Curricular reform in Canada has been moving ahead with the introduction of the new mathematics to earlier grades, further refinement of the teaching of reading through the Initial Teaching Alphabet, and adaptation of courses of study to the particular needs of the mentally retarded, the slow learner and the physically and emotionally handicapped. In the realm of social studies more attention has been given to current issues and to the study of the community at home and abroad. The student drive for studies relevant to the real world has been felt throughout the schools. The Canadian Studies Foundation, a privately sponsored and financed organisation, took on the task of increasing the attention paid to Canadian studies in the schools, colleges and universities. This organisation came into existence after A. B. Hodgett's study *What Culture? What Heritage?* had revealed that the study of Canada and its culture was sadly and tragically neglected. As was incisively stated by the author:

> Most Canadian studies, as currently prescribed and taught, do not nurture advanced intellectual skills, they do not transfer knowledge that is useful to the individual as a citizen or to his society, and they do not encourage an understanding and appreciation of a great many aspects of our cultural heritage.

The Canadian Studies Foundation has been engaged in establishing regional groups across Canada to produce study materials for the correction of these errors.

Other curricular innovations include the development of programmed instruction courses, film loops covering a wide variety of topics from physical education to biology and the development of packaged programmed units designed to contribute to the independent study skills of elementary and secondary school students. Considerable attention, too, has recently been given to reducing the number of American-produced textbooks used in Canadian schools, but this effort has to some degree been obviated by the fact that Canadian publishing houses have practically all been taken over by American firms. One of the main reasons for the widespread use of American-published textbooks is that federal and provincial governments have allowed teaching schedules to become so tight that teachers have not the time to give to writing and to providing a reasonable Canadian content in the curricula of all institutions. Moreover, administrative policies have not provided teachers with sufficient clerical help for routine record-keeping and marking.

INDIANS AND ESKIMOS

Educational provisions for the native Indians and Eskimos have been expanded and modified to a considerable extent, and though by no means ideal do constitute a marked advance over earlier arrangements. An Indian study centre has been established at the universities of British Columbia and Saskatchewan, and Metis studies are under way in Manitoba. These institutions recognise that the educational needs of the Indians, Eskimos and Metis of Canada are unique and people interested in teaching these native peoples require special training. The University of Alberta provides for liaison between its teacher-education courses in Alberta and those in the Northwest Territories in order to bring about an improvement in instruction for native Indians and Eskimos. The federal Department of Indian Affairs and Northern Development has been helping in the production of textbooks and curricular materials specially designed for the native peoples. Some of these materials have been prepared in the native dialects to facilitate transition to the prevailing culture. Another development has been the integration of Indian students into the regular classes of the schools, thus departing from the former practice of segregating native Indian students in their own schools on reserves. Many of the latter still continue but should in time disappear. The practice, too, of having Indian students educated in their own residential schools is also being phased out, although again some will be retained as special-purpose and particular vocational schools. Part Two of the 1967 report entitled *Contemporary Indians of Canada*, prepared by H. B. Hawthorn with the assistance of Joan Ryan, M. A. Tremblay and Frank Vallu, made recommendations to improve the educational opportunities and achievements of the Indian peoples of Canada:

All school authorities should recognize that special and remedial programs are required for the education of Indian children whether under integrated or other auspices.
The expectations of teachers and school authorities should be based on the practical rule that the range of potential intellectual capacity of Indian children is the same as that of white children. Educational programs should take into account the obvious differences in background of the Indian student and also the often less obvious differences in values and motivations.
Teachers should be encouraged to learn as much as possible about the background and culture of their Indian students and should take the initiative in getting to know individuals.

G

Several of these and related measures have been implemented though many remain. However, the directions of reform have been indicated.

Coupled with these reforms is the re-examination of the image of the Canadian Indian as portrayed in textbooks and literature with a view to removing previously cultivated prejudicial and derogatory statements. The image of Canadian Indians in children's literature as either noble savages or thieves, or worse, is giving way to a more realistic appreciation of their individual worth. The individuality of the Eskimos is also being recognised by the government, which is changing the practice of identifying them by number and identifying them by name. There is a general trend to accord different cultures their place in the sun.

REFORMS IN ADMINISTRATION

The concepts governing the administration of schools, colleges and universities have been undergoing considerable change in recent years. Whereas it was formerly the practice to vest all responsibility for the conduct of affairs in the head of the school or department, this is giving way to a sharing of responsibility by a broadly representative committee, and by appointing several people in rotation to the office of principal, dean or president over a period of years. Most institutions still appoint a head for an unspecified number of years, but even here provision is increasingly being made for a review of tenure. School principals are increasingly being moved from school to school over five-year periods. In elementary and secondary schools teachers' committees are being established to act as advisory bodies to their principal and serve as a bridge between school and community. A further trend has been for school trustees and university boards of governors to seek administrative personnel who have a sound academic background rather than those who have concentrated on purely administrative studies.

INSTITUTES OF TECHNOLOGY

During the course of World War II, the Canadian government discovered that technologically competent people in Canada were relatively few and far between. If Canada was to keep abreast of scientific and technological developments, steps had to be taken to correct the situation. Accordingly federal funds were made available to the provincial departments of education for setting up institutes of technology; the provinces of Ontario, Alberta and Manitoba were among the first to do so. British Columbia and others followed later. Students attending these schools are able to study carpentry, industrial drafting, plumbing, refrigeration, data processing, electronics, nursing, pipefitting, dressmaking, navigation, bilingual stenography, chemical technology, technical drawing, to name some of the many possibilities. Candidates for places must have high-school credentials, but provision is made for obtaining these should a would-be candidate lack them.

A NATIONAL OFFICE OF EDUCATION

One of the major problems attending educational reform in Canada is the absence of an office of education at the federal level. The establishment of such an office would make it possible to collate and distribute information about educational developments in Canada and elsewhere and thus help in keeping education everywhere abreast of social and scientific developments. As it is at present, the federal government's *Information Canada* and *Statistics Canada* record and distribute statistical data which is often too late to be of any benefit in either planning or shaping policy. Canada at the moment is one of the few countries in the world without a central body capable of providing an overview of the national scene and seeing this in the perspective of international developments. The Canadian Council of Ministers of Education is but an appendix of the Canadian Education Association. Both are provincially oriented despite the fact that they appear to be national organisations. Their executive organs are manned in the main by officials of provincial departments of education, elected and appointed, with token representation only from other sectors of the educational establishment. As a result there is a serious lack of planning for education that has anything more than provincial boundaries in mind and this at a time when there is critical need for a national perspective on education and a recognition that international interests need also to be served. The British North America Act of 1867 accorded to the provinces exclusive jurisdiction in the realm of education, but there is a growing realisation that this exclusiveness is no longer realistic or reasonable. It remains for some enlightened provincial politicians to come forward and declare their readiness to share their responsibility for education officially with the federal government and make this visible and viable in a federal Office of Education. Reforms could then move forward more rapidly. The idea of a federal office has been endorsed by various organisations including the Canadian School Trustees Association as well as by many who participated in the several Canadian Conferences on Education, during the sixties and is generally recognised as essential to the proper development of education. However, until provincial and federal politicians in office are prepared to put the interests of the future of Canada ahead of their own or party political interests the lack of a federal office will continue to jeopardise Canada's educational image abroad. Canadian educational creativity will continue to suffer and Canadian innovation will continue to be a pale imitation of practice elsewhere.

THE PUBLIC FORUM

Public interest in education is cultivated as much by the issues which are debated in the press and on radio and television as by the bread-and-butter questions which children and young people bring home to the dinner table. A scanning of some of the headlines which appear in the Canadian press from time to time reveals that education is now considered newsworthy. 'Education Expert

Raps Victorianism', 'Diefenbaker to get Request for Education Departments', 'New Roles for Schools Urged', 'Parents Hope to Organize Low-Cost Free School in City', 'Waldorf Schools Ready to Teach "Whole Man" ', 'Schools Break Up Indian Families', 'Eskimos Education called Inadequate', 'Northern Schools having little luck with Desegregation', 'Chinese in Classroom, English in School Yard', 'School Texts Scanned for Bias'. These indicate the extent to which schools and their practice are subjected to public debate and criticism. In most instances the headlines report debates on educational issues which have flowed from public meetings or documents and which have commanded considerable public attention. The story behind each of the headlines is the story of the public's involvement in education.

EDUCATIONAL RESEARCH AND DEVELOPMENT

The growth and development of Canada's educational system was for long hampered by a lack of research into the educative processes within the system. Departments of education, in particular, were negligent in their support of research and where they did establish research divisions within the departmental structure the work done was limited essentially to dealing with practical and administrative problems. Federal and provincial political personnel were too long accustomed to relying upon outside sources such as the United States, Britain, and Europe for basic and applied research, with the result that very little was directly relevant to the Canadian educational scene.

Attempts to rectify this situation have taken the form of establishing such research-oriented bodies as the Alberta Educational Research Council, the Atlantic Institute of Education, the British Columbia Educational Research Council (later the Educational Research Institute) and the Ontario Institute for Studies in Education. This last institute was the best financed, by a forward-looking provincial government, although the Alberta Council also received very good support both from its university and its trustees associations. The Quebec government helped finance educational research through its faculties of education, as well as maintaining a very good research division within its department of education; in many ways the Quebec government has encouraged educational research much beyond that found elsewhere in Canada. In British Columbia the Educational Research Institute, which was given considerable financial support by provincial organisations of teachers and trustees, though not by the government of the day, went into decline as a result of a lack of realistic leadership and a surfeit of unrealistic research.

A newly elected government, socialistic in orientation, has changed this policy and provided the Institute with over $100,000.

Despite these and related problems there has been an increase in the amount of research bearing upon Canadian education, stemming primarily from faculties of education but also from arts and science faculties, where students engage in research for their master's and doctoral degrees. It is unfortunate that the exclusive jurisdiction for education possessed by the provinces seriously limits, even if it does not entirely exclude, federal promotion and support of needed educational research. The federal government can and does contribute heavily to research in the arts, sciences, and the humanities but is reticent about doing so directly in education. Much more needs to be done in this realm and it would be well if the provincial governments saw fit to permit the federal government do what they themselves are unwilling or unable to do—in the interests of Canada.

ALTERNATIVE EDUCATION

People continue to seek alternatives to present modes of education. Free schools constitute an attempt by various groups in society to bring about change in the process of education, change designed to avoid the lock-step and bureaucratic procedures of the traditional school whether public or private. Many of these schools find it possible to provide a freer learning atmosphere for their children than usually obtains, particularly at the elementary level, and sometimes at the secondary-school stage also. These free schools have had an effect on the regular schools, since now the latter have begun to introduce schedules which permit more liberal arrangements of studies, allowing students to attend such classes as they themselves think necessary, to set their own achievement goals and to take examinations and assessments at their own convenience.

The results of these freer arrangements have been impressive and relatively few abuses have attended their introduction. Among the strongest opponents of these experiments have been conservative parents and school boards who have felt that learning depends upon the student adhering steadfastly to strict rules and regulations. But there is mounting evidence that many students are sufficiently motivated to learn without compulsion. Indeed the compulsory school laws are themselves being called in question as perhaps no longer as necessary as they once were.

Essentially the free schools are sponsored by parents who believe that the regulations and curriculum of the regular schools are far too restrictive of the growth and development of the talents of their children. Paradoxically these schools are anything but free; the fees tend to be quite high because relatively few children attend and because the basic costs for operating the school, including paying the teachers' salaries, are more or less fixed. Difficulties which attend the schools, in addition to the high costs per student, include the retention of teachers, the limited programme of studies they can offer, and the tendency for parents to transfer their children back to the public school because of its relative stability. The free schools, nevertheless, continue to survive since they meet the need of those children who for one reason or another do not adjust readily to the regular school and who require a somewhat freer atmosphere. However, with the development of open areas and a more relaxed climate in regular schools, free schools may soon no longer have a market.

In addition to the number of free schools established by dissident youth and disenchanted parents, there are the specialised types of school which are promoted from time to time. The international Outward Bound concept, which seeks to teach self-reliance, leadership and confidence through attaching special emphasis to rigorous outdoor exercises, has been incorporated in a co-educational school for secondary students; it is expensive and makes its appeal to a limited population. The Waldorf school system has also been receiving attention in Canada. This starts with the child at about four years of age and pursues an integrationist philosophy designed to produce the whole man. This is done through having the child continue with one teacher for at least two hours a day throughout the first eight years of schooling, following which specialised teachers take over for the remaining years, through to grade 12. Again, this system makes its appeal to a limited number of parents who want special attention for their offspring.

Then there are those within the regular school system who advocate a new role for the schools beyond the present prepare-for-work philosophy: they are to prepare for life through emphasising learning skills, appreciation of values, skill in making choices and skill in relating to other people. There are also advocates of all-year schools for the purpose of making better use of school buildings and equipment and telescoping the number of years of attendance at school. This idea has made very little headway in Canada except for one or two experiments.

BILINGUALISM AND BICULTURALISM

In 1969 the federal government announced plans for federal aid to bilingual education amounting to $50 million. The central purpose of this programme was to help provinces willing to allow minority language instruction to provide secondary language teaching in majority schools. This was a recognition that the teaching of French primarily, but the languages of other sectors of the population as well, had been neglected. The reception accorded this announcement was mixed. Manitoba responded

by extending its already well-developed French language programme to include Ukrainian, German and other languages.
Ontario moved to establish an all-French language secondary
school, to extend its French language teaching throughout the
system, and to recognise minority languages on a selective and
population basis. British Columbia, on the other hand, remained
essentially unresponsive to this call for Canadian unity beyond
allowing one or two classes in essentially small French communities. The provinces of Alberta, Saskatchewan and those of the
Atlantic seaboard made a variety of provisions for accommodating
the extension of teaching additional languages. On the whole,
and with essentially one exception, the provincial educational
systems recognised the political and cultural validity of a policy
of bilingualism and biculturalism though many of the larger
ethnic groups in Canada understandably favoured a policy of
multiculturalism thereby emphasising the fact that, in addition
to French and English, there were many linguistic groups in
Canada that had helped build the country.

MULTICULTURALISM

Canadians of various ethnic origins operate a variety of schools
for their children. The 66-year-old Chinese public school in
Victoria teaches the basics of the Chinese language, culture and
history to approximately a hundred students who attend between
4 pm and 6 pm, after they have completed their regular public-
school sessions from 9 to 3.30. The students range in age between
six and twelve and attend grades 1–6. Their lessons are concerned
with written and spoken Chinese, history, songs and folk dances,
transmitting Chinese culture to the youth of the Chinese
community and acquainting them with their value systems.
Schools following a similar pattern are to be found among other
ethnic groups, including the Jews, the Mennonites, the Japanese,
and the Ukrainians. In each instance the purpose is to teach
young people of the ethnic group the culture and language
of their forbears and thus to preserve the traditions of their

H

people. All these schools see their role as complementary to the regular public schools and in no way competitive. Some ethnic groups have enough young people to be able to maintain a day school, in which case an attempt is made to combine the academic offerings of the regular school with those of their own cultural studies. These day schools have problems in remaining viable since students tend to stay only until they have completed their elementary studies, teachers tend to come and go frequently since salaries and conditions are not conducive to a lifetime career there, and costs must be borne by the family and the community. However, as long as the public-school system continues to ignore the cultures of the constituent population these schools will continue. One way of reconciling the educational needs of all cultures in Canada would be for the public school, both elementary and secondary, to provide a series of elective studies having to do with the languages, literatures and histories of the cultures which make up the Canadian mosaic.

This mosaic is reflected in the number of immigrants who come to Canada and bring with them the value systems of their country of origin, values which in most instances include respect and desire for education. The accompanying table is indicative of the multicultural character of Canada.

Principal Sources of Immigration 1946–71

Britain	903,979	West Indies	78,089
Italy	468,695	China	56,690
West Germany	265,637	Ireland	45,053
United States	283,792	Austria	39,085
Netherlands	170,839	Czechoslovakia	38,098
Poland	134,351	Australia	40,576
Greece	98,769	Russia	32,150
France	85,285	Belgium	31,909
Yugoslavia	85,925	Denmark	30,075
Portugal	92,444		
Hungary	67,163	TOTAL	3,523,721

Source: *Quick Canadian Facts, 1972–3*

THE EDUCATIONAL HERITAGE

Canada's skills-only immigration policy made it possible in 1967 to attract to its technical and professional work force 4,000 engineers, 1,300 physical scientists, 2,000 professors and principals, 5,400 schoolteachers, 1,200 doctors and 4,300 graduate nurses, as well as 800 artists, writers, and musicians. In the ten-year period 1946–55 the total number of immigrants with professional standing was 44,500. By the same token immigration from Canada to the United States is indicated by figures for the years 1957–64 when a total of 366,129 left for the States of which number 247,788 were native Canadians. During the same period 6,034 Canadians entered the United States from elsewhere.

The flow of talent in and out of Canada may be looked upon as a healthy kind of import-export trade of human resources. On the other hand it makes it difficult to assess the intellectual and cultural component which enters into creating a distinctive pattern of Canadian culture. Certainly the effect of this in-and-out flow on the educational systems of the country is marked by a wide variety of expectations and aspirations. All this has contributed to a kind of identity crisis both in the body politic and in its educational institutions. Thus, Arnold Edinborough writes:

> Several of our newer universities have departments of political science and economics, even history, staffed by Americans. That they were never taught about Canadian institutions in say, Montana or Wyoming or Kansas, we can understand. But if they come up here they can't teach what they don't know. The Canadian component therefore, of our social studies curriculum is very thin indeed in some universities. In English departments the situation is worse. We have not only American professors, bearing the torch for Thoreau, Emerson, Whitman and Hawthorne, but a large number of English professors who, while they know a lot about Wordsworth, Milton and Tennyson, know little about Lampman, Carman or even Leacock—and care less.
>
> In the social sciences, therefore, the Canadian student is likely to have little or no instruction in precisely those things that make this

country a different entity from the U.S. and from the countries from which we sprang.

Again Edinborough writes:

> It is all very well for the government to get tough with the American in matters of trade. It is all very elevating when the Canadian Radio-Television Commission tells radio and television stations to operate on 60% Canadian content or else lose their license. But where is the Canadian content to come from if all through school children are told, either subtly or directly that there is no valid tradition of writing in this country, that their models all lie outside our territorial boundaries?
>
> > Arnold Edinborough, 'There's Something We've Forgotten in Our Schools: Canada', *The Financial Post* (12 September 1970)

From the foregoing it is easy to discern that Canada's educational systems are having difficulty in conserving and transmitting the Canadian heritage. Since a desirable balance between intellectual imports and exports would be such as to strengthen the continuity of Canada's emergent culture, both federal and provincial governments must provide the leadership necessary to ensure youth their heritage.

Canada's heritage is the mosaic of its peoples, who throughout its history have brought with them from the four corners of the earth the fruits of their civilisations, the best of their ideals and accomplishments, and made them a part of Canada's way of life. This heritage is now expressed in a multicultural philosophy of life, a view that says to all the world it is possible for people of widely different backgrounds and upbringing to learn to respect one another's mode of life and learn to live together in creative and constructive harmony, a society in which all, regardless of race, creed, colour, origin, age or sex can have a sense of belonging. It is this heritage, this culture, this multiculture which, moulded in the classrooms of the nation, has emerged as Canada's contribution to its own and the world's people. Hopefully, leaders in government, business, industry and particularly in education will recognise and continue to cultivate this heritage, to ensure the youth of Canada and the world a way of life that reflects the aspirations of all mankind for a world of peace and harmony.

Bibliography

Althouse, J. G. *Structure and Aims of Canadian Education* (Toronto: W. J. Gage, 1949)

Andrews, J. H. M. and Brown, A. F. *Composite High Schools in Canada* (Edmonton: University of Alberta, 1959)

Bissell, C. T. (ed). *Canada's Crises in Higher Education* (Toronto: University of Toronto Press, 1957)

Brehaut, W. 'English Influence in Canadian Education' in *Papers: Comparative and International Education Society of Canada* (Toronto: University of Toronto Press, 1968)

Brown, George W. *Building the Canadian Nation* (New York: MacFadden, 1968)

Campbell, Gordon. *Community Colleges in Canada* (Toronto: Ryerson Press, 1971)

Careless, J. M. S. and Brown, R. Craig (ed). *The Canadians, 1867–1967* (Toronto: Macmillan, 1967)

Carter, G. E. *The Catholic Public Schools of Quebec* (Toronto: W. J. Gage, 1957)

Frecker, G. A. *Education in the Atlantic Provinces* (Toronto: W. J. Gage, 1956)

Gillett, Margaret. *A History of Education: Thought and Practice* (Toronto: McGraw-Hill, 1966)

Harris, Robin S. *Changing Patterns of Higher Education in Canada* (Toronto: University of Toronto Press, 1966)

Hodgetts, A. B. *What Culture? What Heritage?* (Toronto: Ontario Institute for Studies in Education, 1968)

Jocobson, J. V. *Education in Canada's Northland* (Ottawa, 1954)

Johnson, F. H. *Brief History of Canadian Education* (Toronto: McGraw-Hill, 1968)

Katz, J. (ed). *Canadian Education Today* (Toronto: McGraw-Hill, 1956)

Katz, J. (ed). *Elementary Education in Canada* (Toronto: McGraw-Hill, 1961)

Katz, J. *Society Schools and Progress in Canada* (Oxford: Pergamon Press, 1969)

Laycock, S. R. *Special Education in Canada* (Toronto: W. J. Gage, 1963)

Lazerte, M. E. *Teacher Education in Canada* (Toronto: W. J. Gage, 1950)

Lloyd, Woodrow S. *The Role of Government in Canadian Education* (Toronto: W. J. Gage, 1959)

Lower, Arthur E. M. *Colony to Nation. A History of Canada* (Toronto: Longmans, Green, 1947)

Macdonald, John B. *Higher Education in British Columbia and a Plan for the Future* (Vancouver: University of British Columbia, 1962)

MacKinnon, Frank. *The Politics of Education* (Toronto: University of Toronto Press, 1960)

Matthews, Robin and Steele, James. *The Struggle for Canadian Universities* (Toronto: New Press, 1969)

Melling, John. *Right to a Future: The Native Peoples of Canada* (Don Mills, Ontario: T. H. Best Co, 1967)

Phillips, Charles G. *The Development of Education in Canada* (Toronto: W. J. Gage, 1959)

Porter, J. *The Vertical Mosaic* (Toronto: University of Toronto Press, 1965)

Shack, Sybil. *Armed With a Primer* (Toronto: McClelland and Stewart Ltd, 1965)

Sheffield, E. F. *Financing Higher Education in Canada* (Ottawa: CUF, 1960)

Skinner, A. F. 'Scottish Influence in Canadian Education' in
    *Papers: Comparative and International Education Society of
    Canada* (Toronto: University of Toronto Press, 1968)
Statistics Canada *Education in Canada's Northland* (Ottawa:
    Queen's Printer, 1972)

Acknowledgements

Thanks to my wife Mary Evelyn Katz for perceptive patience while I wrote and thanks to my publisher for skilful editorial assistance. Neither is responsible for my errors.

JK

Index

114